When Mormons Doubt

A Way to Save Relationships
and Seek a Quality Life

For Leo and Linus—
that you might grow in truth, beauty, and goodness

Contents

Introduction

TRUTH, BEAUTY, AND GOODNESS

"As long as you live, keep learning how to live."
—SENECA

Tensions in Utah

The writer Alain de Botton had just published his book *Religion for Atheists*, and he knew one thing for certain: He wasn't going to visit Utah on his book tour.

After all, why would Mormons care about a book for nonbelievers? Why would they read something that says atheists should embrace the positive aspects of religion? Mormons already have religion. They wouldn't want to read about it from the perspective of a nonbeliever.

His book simply wouldn't sell in Utah.

Right?

Imagine de Botton's surprise when he discovered that book sales were eight times higher in Utah than in any other state.

In a radio interview, de Botton explained his theory for the booming book sales. He suggested that there are people in Utah who love parts of Mormonism but struggle with many of its public stances and truth claims. Often these people are so unsettled that they leave the fold, distancing themselves from friends and family.

This trend is a major source of cultural tension in Utah right now, as well as throughout the global Mormon community. As sales of *Religion for Atheists* suggest, the tensions are more widespread than we might think.

I've wrestled with these tensions myself.

My wrestling started more than a decade ago, while I served as a Mormon missionary in California. Through conversations with investigators, I discovered things about Church history I hadn't heard of before—that Joseph Smith looked into a hat to translate the Book of Mormon, that he had nearly three dozen wives, and that his translation of the Book of Abraham differs from the papyrus on which it was based.

If I didn't know these things, what else didn't I know? I felt anxious. I told my mission president I was struggling, but he wasn't interested in discussing the details. He said my questions would be sorted out in the afterlife.

I wrote home, asking for help. First, I confided in my dad. He sent me a book that addressed difficult questions about Mormon history. Next, I wrote my favorite high school teacher, a mentor of mine who happened to be a non-Mormon. She told me that because I had committed to serve a mission, I should finish and worry about my troubling questions when I returned.

Although I continued to struggle, these answers were enough to quiet most of my concerns for the rest of my time in California.

It's strange, but when I returned home from my mission and started college at Brigham Young University, my worries about Mormonism faded. I focused on school, work, and dating. I shelved my religious questions and stopped talking about Church history altogether. I was satisfied with simply being Mormon. I started graduate school and got married. Everything seemed fine.

Then my youngest sister left the Church. She had been studying world religions in college and had read several books that caused her to doubt the truth claims of Mormonism. As a result, she decided that organized religion wasn't for her.

My parents were heartbroken. My extended family was heartbroken. My sister's former Primary teachers, Young Women's leaders, and bishops—they too were heartbroken.

Not long after, my best friend from high school also left the Church for similar reasons. The same cycle of heartbreak followed.

I'd had friends leave the Church before, including several when I was in high school. Many of them left partly out of rebellion, a natural teenage response to religion.

But my sister and my best friend weren't like that. In both cases, they weren't leaving because they rejected the commandments of Mormonism, but because after careful research they rejected its truth claims.

To understand their concerns, I dove back into Church history, reading books such as *Rough Stone Rolling*, *Early Mormonism and the Magic Worldview*, *David O. McKay and the Rise of Modern Mormonism*, and so on. I also read official essays[1] on LDS.org that confirmed the validity of what I had read.

All this studying brought back the old anxieties I had experienced on my mission. These weren't simple taunts or red herrings posed by bitter nonbelievers. These were facts supported by official church documents, and yet they inspired sincere doubt.

I wondered how I could reconcile this doubt with my desire to stay united with my believing friends and family. Was there a way to be authentic and still be close to those I loved, even if we had divergent views on Mormonism?

Truth, Beauty, and Goodness

If you have ties to Mormonism, chances are you relate to these issues at some level. Perhaps you have discovered uncomfortable facts about the Church, or perhaps you know someone who has.

Either way, this book is for you.

If you've experienced a faith crisis, this book presents a framework to help you seek a quality life.

If you haven't experienced a faith crisis, this book will help you understand those who have.

The premise of this book is that your ability to save your relationships and seek a quality life depends on your values and beliefs.

If you're an orthodox Mormon, you likely believe that a quality life comes from living the gospel. In practical terms, this often equates to following a list of commandments.

If you're an unorthodox or former Mormon, your beliefs could consist of just about anything. What I fear, however, is that some former Mormons adopt values that are merely the inverse of their prior Mormon beliefs. In such cases, life centers on being the opposite of Mormon—a situation that seems limiting.

I also fear that too many people (including orthodox Mormons) unwittingly buy into the values and beliefs of the surrounding culture. In the United States, this often takes the shape of consumerism: living to buy more stuff, pursue empty distractions, and earn more than our neighbors. Since there's little evidence that consumerism leads to a quality life, I'm hesitant to endorse it.

In this book, I present an alternative view. This view can work for orthodox, unorthodox, and former Mormons alike. It's centered in the pursuit of three universal ideals: truth, beauty, and goodness.

An Ancient Idea

The formal study of truth, beauty, and goodness began a long time ago with philosophers like Socrates, Plato, and Plotinus. Then, like a message in a bottle, it was carried through the ages, finally uncorked and formally named in the fifteenth century by a scholar named Marsilio Ficino.

Since then, the idea has appeared in various places. The philosopher Immanuel Kant wrote three books in the eighteenth century that each covered one of these ideals. Other writers such as W. E. B. Du Bois and C. S. Lewis wrote about them as well. Albert Einstein said the trio was pivotal in his life. He declared, "The ideals which have lighted me on my way and time after time given me new courage to face life cheerfully, have been truth, goodness, and beauty."

What do these words mean in practice, and how are they applicable?

One contemporary description comes from Stephen Covey's book *The 7 Habits of Highly Effective People*. In it, he outlines the importance of what he calls intellectual, spiritual, and social exercise. He also gives examples of what each one looks like in practice.

Intellectual Exercise → "Learning, reading, writing, and teaching"
Spiritual Exercise → "Spending time in nature, expanding spiritual self through meditation, music, art"
Social Exercise → "Making social and meaningful connections with others"[2]

In other words:

Intellectual exercise leads us closer to truth.
Spiritual exercise leads us closer to beauty.
Social exercise leads us closer to goodness.

Put succinctly, truth, beauty, and goodness represent right thinking, right feeling, and right doing.[3]

Because our days consist of thinking, feeling, and doing, these three ideals are the building blocks of a quality life. They can also transcend differences of belief and allow us to find common ground.

Of course, listing these ideals is easy work. Truth, beauty, and goodness are vague enough to sound promising without ruffling any feathers. It's only once we begin to unpack them that we discover that the key to a quality life is to find the proper *blend* of these three ideals. And there's nothing easy about that.

Blending Truth, Beauty, and Goodness

We each have a natural tendency to privilege one of these ideals over the others. Most of the time that's perfectly okay. It's how we offer our unique gifts to the world.

However, sometimes we pursue one of these ideals to a fault, and as a result we neglect the other two. When this happens, we lose our ability to live a quality life.

Let's look at how this works, starting with truth.

The pursuit of truth without beauty makes us cynical. Consider the example of a devout Mormon woman who discovers uncomfortable facts about the Church. Her discovery leads her down a rabbit hole of pain and confusion. In the process, she stops turning to sources that once gave her peace and emotional strength. She used to say prayers of gratitude, sing comforting hymns, and ponder devotional texts. Now she spends that time rehashing cold facts and waxing cynical.

Is this a quality life? True, she's better educated (read: armed with more truth), but she lacks the inner peace (or beauty) she once had. She ought to blend her study of the truth with deliberate expressions of gratitude, time in nature, and reading texts that speak to her heart.

The pursuit of truth without goodness makes us lonely. This is the story of Stephen Dedalus, the main character in the novel *A Portrait of the Artist as a Young Man*. As he reaches maturity, Stephen learns that Catholicism, especially as it's practiced in Ireland, is deeply flawed. He leaves his community and disassociates himself from his friends, family, and religion. He even refuses to pray out loud for his mother on her deathbed.

Afterward, Stephen is racked with guilt for what he did to his mother. He grows lonely and despondent, and his choice to reject his community haunts him.

The pursuit of beauty without truth makes us gullible. This happens when people interpret all peaceful feelings as evidence of the truth. At its most extreme, this occurs when people get pulled into pseudoscience and dangerous cults. Such people want to believe that because something feels right, it must be right. However, as Flannery O'Connor once said, "The truth does not change according to our ability to stomach it." Sometimes the truth hurts.

The pursuit of beauty without goodness makes us selfish. This happens when people seek personal ecstasy without the willingness to roll up their sleeves and help the truly needy. It's when self-care turns self-centered.

The pursuit of goodness without beauty is exhausting. It's robotic and perfunctory, born out of duty rather than desire. It's the Mormon checklist, the stats and numbers. It's when every experience feels like "I have to because I have to because I have to…" rather than "I want to."

Finally, the pursuit of goodness without truth is misdirected. For example, Mormons once mistakenly believed that God changed people's skin color based on their worthiness. These Mormons wanted to be good by having faith in their religious authorities, but they were ignorant of the science of skin color. And this ignorance—as is the case with all ignorance—was harmful. Ignorance is bliss only for the ignorant. It hurts everyone else.

***

The end goal isn't to spend exactly one third of our waking minutes focused on each ideal. Again, we each have our own primary passions and our own way of pursuing truth, beauty, and goodness. The goal, then, is to reflect on how well we achieve a blend that works for us, and to keep our personal excesses in check. As the scholar Wayne Booth said, these three ideals "rival one another at the fringe, but in the center they join." Where they join we find a quality life.

A Quality Life versus a Sad Heaven
But is a quality life enough?

Some believers don't think so. They say, "It's easy to talk about living a quality life, but what happens after death? When I die, I want all my family to be in heaven, and those who leave my religion won't be. That's what makes me sad."

This sentiment is a source of sorrow for people all over the world, perhaps especially for Mormons. If it's true, it's devastating. You'll be forever separated from those you love because they don't believe the way you do.

But is it true? Will the faithful spend eternity weeping about their loved ones who didn't get in line with their particular beliefs?

Will believers with a black sheep in their family end up in Sad Heaven?

The author Rob Bell once told a story that calls this idea into question. His Protestant congregation hosted an event where they produced and displayed their own works of art.

One piece was a beautifully rendered quote from Gandhi. Most attendees were moved by the quote, but someone went rogue midway through the evening and placed a note on the piece. It read, "Reality check: He's in hell."

"Gandhi's in hell?" Rob Bell asked when he recounted the story. "And someone knows this for sure? And felt the need to let the rest of us know?" Bell says that we shouldn't be so certain that we know what will happen to others in the afterlife.

Based on how few times I've died, I have to agree. I can't be confident about what will happen in the afterlife.

For instance, I have a friend who grew up in stark poverty, who was introduced to drugs at a young age, and who has struggled with violence for decades. How could I make the case that he'd fare worse in an afterlife than I would? If I'd had his upbringing, I would be in his shoes.

At this point, some Mormons might say that baptisms for the dead will take care of everything. They reconcile Sad Heaven with the belief that everyone will choose Mormonism once they learn about it in the afterlife.

But what about Mormons who reject their religion in this life?

Picture someone who lives a happy, selfless life but who rejects the idea that polygamy was ordained of God. Or imagine someone who deliberately develops their spiritual, intellectual, and social health but who can't believe that Brigham Young was once God's official mouthpiece on the earth. Will these people be banished from heaven, leaving their believing counterparts to suffer forever without them?

Again, I haven't died, so I don't know. But if it turns out that we are judged beyond the grave for our deeds and beliefs in this life, I have reason to think we will find only mercy. After all, there are more than seven billion people on the planet, and only a tiny fraction—around 0.01%—are active Mormons. Similar numbers could be calculated for any number of beliefs, but mercy extends beyond those limits.

Two Wagers: Which Will You Choose?

This conundrum about the afterlife has been a source of tension for centuries. Four hundred years ago a philosopher named Blaise Pascal worried about what would happen to him when he died. After careful consideration, he decided that it was in his best interest to have faith. He figured that if he were right, God would give him an everlasting reward. And if he were wrong, he'd be dead and buried—just like everyone else.

A safe bet, right?

The problem with Pascal's wager is that he believed in a niche version of seventeenth-century Catholicism. As such, he believed in a God who rejected Protestants, Muslims, Buddhists, and so on.

Given that almost no one alive today believes in Pascal's version of Catholicism, we'll all be terribly disappointed in the afterlife if his wager is true. His God might cast us into hell because our beliefs don't measure up.

Luckily there's another wager that's more humane.

I call it Mr. Rogers's wager.

Mr. Rogers made a habit of repeating the line, "I like you just the way you are." It's a simple phrase with a lot of beauty behind it.

The wager works like this: Let's say someone disagrees with your beliefs. Rather than worry about their eternal salvation, you could love them just the way they are.

Some cynics might get the wrong idea when they're told to love people just the way they are. They might think that if they love others in this way, they'll be endorsing bad behavior. But that's not what Mr. Rogers meant.

When Mr. Rogers says he likes me just as I am, I feel like I want to be my best self. This thought is in line with recent studies about how feeling loved might be just the thing people need to stop their unwanted behaviors.[4]

In other words, let's say your mother, daughter, father, son, or sibling no longer believes the way you do. Should you double down on your version of Pascal's wager, holding tightly to the belief that they won't be able to join you in heaven? Or should you double down on pure love, thereby finding commonalities and enjoying their company?

We human beings don't know much. But we know we're alive. What a tragedy it would be, then, to let our fear of the unknown sour the relationships that our happiness hinges upon right now. As Mark Twain said, "There isn't time, so brief is life, for bickerings, apologies, heartburnings, callings to account. There is only time for loving, and but an instant, so to speak, for that."

A Way to Save Relationships and Live a Quality Life
I sometimes meet Mormons who believe that a quality life is defined exclusively by Mormon milestones. "My kids all went on missions, married in the temple, and pro-

duced lots of grandchildren," they might say. But these events don't necessarily indicate a quality life. Going on a mission, marrying in the temple, and having children—these milestones have the veneer of success but not necessarily the substance.

A better measure is whether we're pursuing the proper blend of truth, beauty, and goodness. This measure works inside or outside of any religion. It can help believers and nonbelievers look at every belief system (including Mormonism) with as much objectivity as possible, holding onto what is true, beautiful, and good—and dropping what isn't. If we do this earnestly, we'll move upward no matter what we believe about the afterlife.

It's my hunch that everyone intuitively believes this. We also recognize that truth, beauty, and goodness are worthwhile even when they come from a source that doesn't belong to our tradition. Whether it's a scientific fact, a moving piece of music, or a chance to volunteer at a homeless shelter, we seek after these things whether they originate inside Mormonism or not.

In short, the common paradigm of success within Mormonism needs to change. Success comes from deliberately seeking the proper blend of truth, beauty, and goodness—regardless of our belief or doubt in Mormonism. If a mixed-belief family can embrace this idea, they'll unite around what matters most and avoid unnecessary heartache.

Ultimately, whether your loved ones are believers or nonbelievers, chances are you still share more similarities than differences when it comes to these ideals. Once you look for those similarities and add a dose of compromise, you'll find ways to develop spiritual, intellectual, and social health together. Daughters, sons, brothers, sisters, wives, husbands, parents, and grandparents. Perhaps you'll talk all night about your favorite books, spend time together in nature, serve in a local homeless shelter— anything but focus relentlessly on your differences.

Will this new definition of success completely erase the divide between believers and nonbelievers?

Perhaps not.

But it can help us in our efforts to save our relationships and seek a quality life.

In the following chapters I explore each of the three ideals, starting with beauty, to show how they can help us find common ground despite differences of belief.

Beauty, Part 1

A CALM SO DEEP

"Everything has beauty, but not everyone sees it."
—CONFUCIUS

A Struggle to Find the Words

I had never seen so much blood as the night our second child was born.

It didn't work out the way we wanted. The doctors could see from the monitor that the baby's heart rate plummeted every time my wife had a contraction, signifying that he was being strangled by the umbilical cord.

Each drop electrified my nerves.

I spent the hours of labor thinking that our baby was either going to be born with severe brain damage or that he would die before birth.

Eventually the doctors felt it was necessary to do a C-section. My wife was wheeled into the operating room and cut open. Her blood drained into tubes and gathered into bags, compounding my anxiety.

When the baby was born, I couldn't tell if he had suffered brain damage. His cries were strained and choked. I waited for the nurse to clean him off, and then the baby and I were taken to the nursery.

As we settled in, I asked the nurse if everything was okay.

When she said that everything was fine, that the baby was completely healthy and the surgery had gone well, I had a sense of deep relief.

Anxiety was replaced by peace.

I looked at my son squirming in the nursery cradle beside me, and I felt a powerful sense of connection to him. We were both overwhelmed by what had just happened, powerless in the face of nature.

As I sat there, this feeling of connection expanded to all human beings. I felt that at a fundamental level, despite our best efforts to pretend otherwise, we are all weak, scared, and alone. None of us really knows what we're doing, and so there is room only for empathy, forgiveness, and love. In that moment, I felt a deep desire to remove all judgment and just be kind.

This feeling of connection and generosity is familiar to people all over the world, and yet we often struggle to put it into words. In fact, it's almost as though the feeling simply can't be captured in language.

Here are some approximate terms I've heard to describe what it feels like:

An epiphany
A spiritual experience
Love
Unity

Oneness
Awe
The higher emotions
The sublime
Awareness
Pure love
Mindfulness
Beauty

The poet William Wordsworth called it "a calm so deep." The poet Percy Bysshe Shelley said that when you feel it, you will have "a mind inflamed with the desire of benefiting mankind."

The French movie *Amelie* describes the experience as "a strange feeling of absolute harmony ... a surge of love, an urge to help mankind."

Paul of Tarsus said, "The fruit of the Spirit is love, joy, peace, longsuffering, gentleness, goodness, faith, meekness, temperance." And the Book of Mormon says that you experience beauty when you "have no more disposition to do evil, but to do good continually."

As you can see, beauty is a feeling that often leads you toward goodness. And when you practice goodness, you often feel more beauty. It's an upward movement, toward a quality life.

Temporary Blissful Centerings
Wayne Booth, a professor of rhetoric at the University of Chicago, called these moments of beauty "temporary blissful centerings." In the years before he died, he made a list of the times he had experienced such moments.

This is one of the most important documents I've ever read, because it reminds me of what really matters in life. If you take nothing else from this book, I hope you will take ideas from this list and live by them.

Here it is, edited for length: the moments that brought Wayne Booth bliss.

- Loving my lifelong partner
- Cuddling a newborn child or grandchild
- Playing games—with children, with friends, with anybody who is fully engaged with the game
- Listening to powerful music
- Playing music, the supreme bliss
- Reading any novel or poem slowly, deliciously, totally absorbed
- Writing a draft of something that feels good
- Working many hours with marvelously collegial friends
- Teaching a class when the discussion goes right
- Looking at a flower, or a shimmering lake, or a magnified photo of an insect, or a rainbow flash from a prism, feeling a flood of gratitude
- Lighting a well-laid fire…staring at the flames as they mount
- Attending Catholic Mass in a tiny chapel in Flavigny, France, singing the hymns, reveling in the deeply probing sermons by the priest who has welcomed us even though he knows that we are Mormons
- Meditating silently in a Quaker meeting, surrounded by friends who interrupt only infre-

quently to report what their spirit dictates

- Attending the bat and bar mitzvahs of grandkids Emily and Aaron—total "spiritual elevation" or "religious ecstasy"
- Singing the Mormon hymn "Come, Come, Ye Saints" at my missionary homecoming service[1]

These moments of temporary blissful centerings make life worth living. Any of us can experience such moments, so long as we deliberately seek them out and are fully present when they occur. They might happen while you're gardening, painting, hiking—whatever you do to experience beauty.

Fortunately, we don't have to wait for some authority to save us, or the stars to align just right, or a traumatic near-death moment. As Lao Tzu once wrote, "At the center of your being you have the answer." Beauty is always within reach, even in our weakness.

A Kingdom Within

Spiritual traditions all over the world have taught about beauty using metaphors and the language of their time. Buddha taught about awakening, Muhammad taught about submission, and Moses taught about entering the presence of God.

Even if you don't believe in any of these traditions, there is something to learn from each one about how to experience beauty.

For instance, Jesus of Nazareth said that the experience is like entering a heavenly kingdom. He said it's an experience that's available to all people, and he called this message the good news.

We are told that "Jesus traveled about from one town and village to another, proclaiming the good news of the kingdom of God."

When someone asked Jesus, "When will the kingdom of God come?" he responded, "The kingdom of God will not come if you watch for it. Nor will anyone be able to say, 'It is here' or 'It is there.' For the kingdom of God is within you."

Elsewhere, when a scribe agreed with Jesus that love is the most important of all the commandments, Jesus told him, "You are not far from the kingdom of God." Jesus wasn't saying that the man was about to die and go to heaven. Instead, Jesus was saying that in that moment the man was nearing a state of pure love.

The good news, then, is that we don't have to wait until the afterlife to obtain the treasure of abundant living. We can experience it right now. A nineteenth-century philosopher put it this way: "What is 'the good news'? That true life, eternal life, has been found—it is not something promised, it is already here, it is within you: as life lived in love."[2]

The good news is that beauty is all around—always within reach—and you are capable of experiencing it.

Why do we struggle to find it?

Because our minds are overrun with chatter and distraction, possibly to the point of addiction.

Mind Chatter, Distraction, and Addiction

If you're like most people, you feel anxious about the off-putting tasks ahead of you. Perhaps you need to finish a tedious work assignment, get an oil change, or clean your house. Whatever you need to do, your mind keeps reminding you about it.

Perhaps your mind also gives you constant grief about your past mistakes. On an endless loop you hear, "You shouldn't have done that" and "How could you be so clueless?" You know that worrying about your mistake for the seventh time won't fix it, but your mind keeps worrying about it anyway.

This is mind chatter. Anxiety about the future, guilt about the past—these negative thoughts play on repeat in the spools of our minds. Each time they do, we're a step removed from feeling joy and generosity in the present.

We intensify the problem by cluttering our minds with worry. Soon enough, we find ourselves in a downward spiral. We want to turn the chatter off—to quiet the endless loop of anxiety and shame—but we don't know how.

So we turn to distraction. We seek for quick fixes and empty calories. We fill our time with mind-numbing busywork and trivialities: surfing the Web without purpose, binge-watching TV shows, or playing video games for hours on end.

In this way, we momentarily escape our mind chatter.

However, when we're through with mindless distraction, we find that our mind chatter is still there. It might even be louder because we haven't dealt with it in a healthy way.

And so the avalanche begins. The louder our mind chatter, the more aggressively we pursue distraction. As Henry David Thoreau once wrote, "The mass of men lead lives of quiet desperation"—desperate because we know what we should be feeling but can't seem to feel it.

At its worst, distraction gives way to addiction, a state where we compulsively do that which erodes our joy against our best wishes. In this state it becomes harder and harder to find what we want out of life.

We'll never fully overcome our mind chatter, but we can work against it by seeking simple ways to experience beauty. Bit by bit, the raw experience of beauty can change us.

How to Nurture Beautiful Experiences

The nature writer Rachel Carson outlines one way to practice seeing beauty in our daily lives. She says that when we look at something beautiful we should ask, "What if I had never seen this before? What if I knew I would never see it again?"

When I first read these words, I was sitting on a train, passing by a mountain range in Utah Valley. I looked up and imagined myself seeing these mountains for the first time. I realized how breathtaking they were. I then imagined that this would be the last time I ever saw these mountains. I felt grateful to live where I did. These were mountains I had looked at thousands of times in my life, but I had seldom truly experienced them.

We can extend Rachel Carson's question to other experiences. "What if this were the first time you had ever tasted a fresh peach? What if it were the last time you would ever taste it?" Or "What if this were the first time you had ever held the hand of a loved one? What if it were your last time?"

With these simple questions, we can experience life instead of just existing. We can stop multitasking, which is the act of experiencing nothing fully, and start focusing on this moment.

We can also practice experiencing beauty in both our leisure and our work. This is illustrated in the list from Wayne Booth when he mentions a moment from his leisure ("listening to powerful music") right alongside a moment from his work ("teaching a class when the discussion goes right"). Both activities have the capacity to bring beauty into our lives. If they don't, it's a sign we need to change something—either what we do or how we do it.

Personally, I often find beauty in conversation. John O'Donohue, an Irish poet who wrote a book about beauty, talks about experiencing beauty in this way as well. He asks, "When is the last time that you had a great conversation? A conversation that wasn't just two intersecting monologues, which is what passes for conversation often in this culture. When was the last time you had a great conversation in which you overheard yourself saying things that you never knew you knew? … A conversation that continued to sing in your mind for weeks afterwards?"

I also find beauty in mindfulness meditation, a practice that has opened up my capacity to feel a peace so profound I didn't know it was possible. If you're interested in getting started, I offer some suggestions in the endnotes.[3]

Can Ye Feel So Now?

One of the most powerful verses of the Book of Mormon is Alma 5:26, wherein Alma asks, "If ye have experienced a change of heart, and if ye have felt to sing the song of redeeming love, I would ask, can ye feel so now?"

The essence of this question is worthy of reflection, no matter who you are. If you've felt beauty before in your life, do you feel it now?

I once posed this question in a forum of unorthodox Mormons.[4] Specifically, I asked, "Do you feel the Spirit (or the equivalent feeling) more or less than you did when you were orthodox?"

The answers I received helped me reflect on what I might say at this stage in my life. I hope they do the same for you, so I'll list some of the responses here. As you read them, think about how you might respond.

1. "I'm still figuring this out. I think it's about the same for me, but it ebbs and flows."
2. "Meditation and prayer brings the Spirit. ... It's hard to feel the Spirit at church."
3. "I feel that my discouragement may be keeping the Spirit away from me."
4. "I feel the Spirit in different places. When I feel it, it seems deeper. I don't feel it very much at church. I feel it through music and being in nature."
5. "I rarely feel it at church. For some reason, I find it more in music now than ever before."
6. "I'm more conscious of the Spirit in my life in daily ways, and in ways that have nothing to do church."
7. "I feel it less, honestly. Sometimes I worry that maybe I'm like Laman and Lemuel, 'past feeling.' I'm working through that."
8. "Absolutely more. I'm living authentically now."
9. "Whether I feel the Spirit doesn't depend on the

Church for me. It depends on how much I am making myself available to feel it."

10. "Less in sacrament meeting talks. ... More in Primary. More in my dealings with others, because I am desperately trying to be genuinely kinder to everyone I meet."

How would you respond?

Hopefully you experience beauty more often—no matter what your beliefs are.

Yet you shouldn't automatically be troubled if you no longer experience beauty in the same ways you used to. That might just be a sign you're developing in new ways. It's like going back to a movie you liked when you were young and discovering that it doesn't pack the same emotional punch. What brought beauty into your life might not have the same effect as you mature. To develop beyond where you are now, you might have to seek new ways to grow.

The important thing is that you're actively seeking for beauty. Those who seek will find.

Goodness, Part 1

THAT WE MIGHT HAVE JOY

"Vain is the word of the philosopher that does not heal any suffering."

—EPICURUS

Three Stories about Leaving Tradition

1.

A Catholic couple in Utah adopted a baby boy.

They raised him inside the Catholic faith. The spiritual nature of his upbringing resonated strongly with him, and from the time he was young he aspired to the priesthood.

Then he fell in love with a Mormon girl.

As their courtship progressed, he assumed he would easily convert her to Catholicism. Meanwhile, she assumed she would convert him to Mormonism.

As it turned out, she was right. When he was old enough to no longer require his parents' consent, he was baptized as a Mormon. His family was devastated. It's been more than 30 years since his baptism, and his parents are *still* hurt by his decision to convert from Catholicism to Mormonism.

2.

Tevye had three problems, all of them daughters.

His first daughter rejected the husband he chose for her.

His second daughter rejected his politics and married a Marxist.

But then his third daughter did something much worse in his eyes. She rejected Judaism, the religious tradition of her childhood. She married a Christian.

In the moment of crisis, she stood before her father with tears in her eyes, pleading for him to understand her decision.

Tevye listened to her plea and imagined the implications of giving his blessing. "How can I turn my back on my faith—my people?" he asked himself. "If I try and bend that far, I'll break!"

At this, he grew angry. He could understand marrying for love, but marrying outside of the Jewish faith crossed a line. "No!" he shouted. "No! No! No!" Then he left his daughter weeping and alone, informing the rest of his family that she was dead to them from that day on.

3.

Carolyn Jessop was raised by polygamists.

At age 18, she was forced to marry 50-year-old Merril Jessop, a bishop with three wives and more than 30 children.

Over the next 15 years, Carolyn gave birth to eight more of Merril's children. After their first four children, doctors warned that additional pregnancies would endanger Carolyn's life, but her husband got her pregnant four more times anyway. Her eighth and final pregnancy resulted in an emergency hysterectomy, a procedure that saved her life.

Carolyn also witnessed the bizarre cruelty of Warren Jeffs, the prophet in their polygamist sect. While Carolyn lived in Colorado City, Jeffs had every dog in the city slaughtered and all works of fiction burned. By his decree, any boy caught flirting with a girl was cast out of the community. Many of these boys were forced to hitchhike alone on the freeway to find a new place to live.

At age 35, Carolyn had enough. She escaped with all eight of her children, driving them to a safe house in Salt Lake City. She was granted full custody in a matter of months.

However, Carolyn's oldest daughter, Betty, hated their new life. She was devastated by her mother's choice to leave the fold and was certain that her mother was bound for hell. More than anything, Betty wanted to return to her faith and her upbringing. When she turned 18, she went back to the polygamists.

To most people, this reaction is baffling. Why, after witnessing so much dysfunction and abuse, did she choose to return?

Her response?

"I just couldn't deny what was in my heart, my belief in my religion," she said.

The World's Second Oldest Tradition

These three stories—the first from a man in my neighborhood, the second from *Fiddler on the Roof*, and the third from Carolyn Jessop's book *Escape*—explore the tensions that emerge between tradition and change.

There are millions of similar stories—some more extreme and heart wrenching, some less so. But they each have one thing in common. In every case, when people reject the traditions of their loved ones, their loved ones feel pain. That's the way it's always been.

Breaking from tradition is the world's second oldest tradition.

If someone you love has left your tradition, you might be tempted to think that your life is a failure. You failed to keep someone in the fold. Maybe you blame yourself or think that you should have been more faithful.

And yet everyone knows that leaving a tradition isn't inherently bad.

Somewhere in your ancestry *someone* broke from tradition to give you the traditions you enjoy today. And all sorts of people—especially Mormons—get excited when someone leaves another tradition to join their own.

How do we know whether the decision to break from tradition is good or bad? Most people would say that Tevye's story isn't as devastating as Carolyn Jessop's story, but do we know why? What measure do we use to define what is good?

Seeking an Inclusive Definition of Goodness

When my best friend from high school told me he was leaving the Church, I said I worried about people who pursued that path. I said that in my experience, people who left the Church seemed worse off than those who stayed. Some became consumed with drugs and drinking, some stopped living a life centered in service, many were bitter, etc. I told my friend that I wanted to move upward, not downward, and so I wasn't interested in leaving Mormonism.

Since that time, I've realized that reality is more complex than I'd thought. It turns out that if you strictly define goodness by your worldview, then you will *always* say that those who abandon it are worse off. You will always view those who leave your tradition in a negative light, as illustrated by the stories above.

Still, I can't shake the idea that my concerns about leaving Mormonism have some validity. I say this because I've seen the religion bring goodness into people's lives. I've seen Mormons visit the sick, bring food to ward members who've recently had babies, help people move out of their homes, etc. It's a pragmatic, earthy religion that employs a healthy sense of volunteerism. As such, Mormonism offers a lot of goodness to the world.

To resolve this tension, we need a definition of goodness that can work for Mormons *and* former Mormons. This way we can applaud the best aspects of Mormonism without automatically labeling those who leave as morally depraved.

One useful definition of goodness surfaced around 2,300 years ago with the Greek philosopher Epicurus.

Epicurus wanted to find the essence of a happy life. He watched his fellow citizens seek fame, wealth, and the favor of the gods. And yet he saw that none of those pursuits guaranteed happiness. The famous craved more fame, the wealthy craved more wealth, and those who sacrificed goats to the gods were still terrified that the gods would punish them.

Epicurus therefore advised his fellow citizens not to live for external rewards but to seek abiding happiness, which he referred to as tranquility, or inner peace. He believed that reaching inner peace depends on your ability to follow two rules:

1. Seek pleasure, except where pleasure leads to greater pain.
2. Avoid pain, except where pain leads to greater pleasure.[1]

It's a simple but profound formula, one that can serve as a guidepost for every decision you make in life. That is, you must weigh your choices against the pleasure and pain you will experience afterwards. To do this, you must practice prudence.

Those who read Epicurus perpetuated principles from his philosophy. The Roman slave Epictetus wrote that when faced with a pleasure, you should first consider "how long you will enjoy the pleasure, and also how long you will afterwards revile yourself."[2] And the philosopher Seneca, who frequently quoted Epicurus, wrote that "above all, make this your business: learn how to feel joy."[3]

Learn how to feel joy.

To echo a Mormon verse: You are that you might have joy.

Of course, what brings you joy depends on who you are.

You might seek pleasure by watching one episode of your favorite show tonight instead of binge watching it. After all, you don't want to revile yourself when you wake up with a TV hangover.

Or you might choose to train for a marathon because it brings you joy to reach new levels of health and endurance. As Epicurus said, "The greater the difficulty, the more the glory in surmounting it."

In this same vein, you might choose to sacrifice deeply for a cause you believe in. As George Bernard Shaw said, "This is the true joy in life, the being used for a purpose recognized by yourself as a mighty one."[4] Your mighty purpose could be creating beautiful art, advocating for social reform, or serving the needy in your neighborhood. Whatever it is, you will find that sacrifice leads to greater pleasure—what Shaw calls true joy.

In short, this formula from Epicurus gets at the heart of goodness. It fits with a range of helpful models for morality, including the golden rule and the concept of duty. When we treat other people as we would want to be treated, we're more likely to find tranquility and inner peace.

This formula from Epicurus also shows us why all breaks from tradition aren't equally good or bad, even though they all cause pain. Compare Carolyn Jessop's situation to Tevye's. In both cases, their daughters broke from tradition, but the choices they made don't seem morally equivalent in light of Epicurus's formula. One daughter returned to an abusive sect. The other daughter married a kind and earnest Christian. We can't know for sure, but one of these choices seems more damaging to a person's long-term tranquility.

In this manner, Epicurus's formula gives us a way to talk about goodness across cultures and beliefs.

And yet some people might say that this formula is too vague to be useful. They might say that it only states the obvious: that we should be happy. But it doesn't tell us exactly how to be happy.

To a degree, these critics are right. The formula doesn't give us a precise list of actions that everyone should follow to find inner peace.

That's because, unlike truth, goodness is not a hard science.

Instead, goodness is a soft science. It interprets a collection of human behavior and feelings, which are hard to quantify in a lab. [5]

We discover what is good through our experiences and through the experiences of other people. We might avoid certain behaviors because they've negatively affected our tranquility in the past. And we might purposely avoid certain behaviors because we've seen how they've negatively affected the tranquility of others. This is perhaps the best reason to study literature, history, and the social sciences. They teach us how to live so we never have to experience certain sorrows ourselves.[6]

Three Mormon Commandments

Before I end this chapter, I'd like to look at a few examples of how orthodox, unorthodox, and former Mormons might be able to agree on specific ways to be good. To do this, I'll look at how Epicurus's formula relates to three Mormon commandments, starting with prayer.

Prayer

There's an old joke about two rabbis. One night after dinner they discuss the existence of God at length, eventually arriving at the conclusion that God does not exist.

The next morning, one of the rabbis wakes up and can't find his friend. He looks everywhere in the house and then decides to search for him outside in the garden.

There he finds his friend saying his ritual prayers.

"What are you doing?" he says.

"As you can clearly see," says his friend, "I am saying my ritual morning prayers."

"But last night we talked at length and decided that God does not exist. Why would you wake up to say your prayers as usual?"

Then his friend replies, a bit puzzled, "What does God have to do with it?"

It's a joke, but it's also wise. It invites us to consider the benefits of our spiritual traditions. Specifically, it asks us to evaluate what we get from a ritual such as prayer.

For Mormons, prayer consists of at least two components—giving thanks and asking for help.

Giving thanks brings happiness into the present. Having a set time each day (or multiple times each day) where you express gratitude is a powerful way to build joy. When you are earnestly thankful for what you have, your misery dissolves.

Asking for help in prayer can also be a useful way to visualize what you want to achieve in the future. The ritual of prayer—pausing your other activities, closing your eyes, focusing your attention—helps you picture what you really want. From there you can better achieve what you really want instead of drifting from urgent task to urgent task throughout the day.

According to Epicurus's formula, certain features of prayer are worth holding onto because they lead to greater pleasure, even for nonbelievers. Believers may find power in appealing to the Divine for guidance, but we can all benefit from moments of stillness. We can all benefit from deliberate moments of gratitude and visualization.

The Word of Wisdom

The Word of Wisdom has been interpreted in dozens of ways over the years, but for contemporary Mormons it's mostly about avoiding tea, coffee, cigarettes, alcohol, and hard drugs.

You don't have to be Mormon to know that the Word of Wisdom has merit. People who have never been Mormon write essays such as "What I Learned Not Drinking for Two Years" and "No Alcohol, No Coffee for 15 Months" to describe how their lives are better without the excesses of alcohol. Non-Mormon works of fiction such as *The Adventures of Huckleberry Finn*, *Requiem for a Dream*, and *Boyhood* deal with these themes as well. Caution against substance abuse isn't a Mormon invention.

Mormons and former Mormons might disagree about whether it's okay to drink a cup of coffee or a glass of wine, but they can agree on the dangers of excess. That is, they can agree with Seneca when he said, "pleasure, unless it has been kept within bounds, tends to rush headlong into the abyss of sorrow." That is a line worth living by.

The Law of Chastity
Sexual morality can also be guided by Epicurus's formula, especially in regards to marital fidelity.

Again, this principle isn't limited to Mormonism. Pursuing momentary sexual pleasure heedless of consequences often leads to long-term pain. Think of John Edwards, who cheated on his dying wife; Anthony Weiner, whose sexual antics humiliated his spouse; Bill Cosby, whose violent lust victimized dozens of women; and on and on.

A certain level of sexual restraint leads to greater happiness for you, your partner, and your children. Mormons and non-Mormons can agree on the value of delayed gratification and mindful sexuality even if they disagree about the specifics of what it means for them. The point is to not let your desire for pleasure inflict long-term pain on yourself and those you love.

Epicurus's formula also highlights why so many people take issue with the Mormon stance on homosexuality. Many have seen firsthand that gays and lesbians aren't happier when they're told that loving someone of the same sex is a sin. They know that attempts to change someone's sexual orientation lead to misery. They follow the line "wickedness never was happiness" to its logical conclusion—if you are happy, you must not be wicked—and know that gays and lesbians aren't happier in context of Mormon views on sexuality.

***

I could keep listing examples that illustrate the relationship between pleasure, pain, and goodness. The point is that we can use Epicurus's formula to decide which habits bring us joy and which ones don't. This might seem radical to some orthodox Mormons, but it's worth noting that at a certain level, we all pick and choose our favorite rules and ignore or downplay others. It's human. We're all doing our best to hold to the things we hope will make us joyful.

In conclusion, I'd like to circle back to Epicurus's formula:

1. Seek pleasure, except where pleasure leads to greater pain.
2. Avoid pain, except where pain leads to greater joy.

Throughout this chapter, I've focused a lot on avoiding pain as a way to find joy. But avoiding pain is only one half of the formula. The other half, as you can see, is to seek pleasure. We *should* seek pleasure, especially when it inspires feelings of beauty. And— so long as the pursuit doesn't result in greater pain— we shouldn't feel guilty for it.

We should do things that bring us delight, and we should be fully present so we can actually take delight in them. As the philosopher Soren Kierke- gaard noted, "Most men pursue pleasure with such breathless haste that they hurry past it."[7] If we want to be happy, if we want to practice goodness, we can't hurry past pleasure. After all, whether it comes from watching a sunset or sacrificing for a mighty purpose, we're here to have joy.

Truth, Part 1

OH SAY, WHAT IS TRUTH?

"The truth knocks on the door and you say, 'Go away, I'm looking for the truth,' and so it goes away."

—ROBERT PIRSIG

How to Make Babies

It wasn't until fifth grade that I learned the truth about baby making.

I was in music class singing with my classmates when, without prompting, my friend Josh turned to me and asked if I knew how babies were made.

"Of course I know," I said, hoping he would drop the subject.

"How?" he asked.

"Uhh...you have to be married and then you kiss," I said.

Josh laughed. "Are you serious?"

When I told him I was serious, he proceeded to tell the rest of the kids sitting at the table what I'd said. They laughed nervously.

Because I have a natural idiocy about me, I stood my ground. "If that's not how it works, then how does it?"

When Josh explained it to me, I knew he was right. I won't bore you (or excite you!) with the details. I'll just say he was right.

Later that day, a few more of my classmates found out what I'd said and mocked me for believing something so stupid. Babies come from kissing? Ha!

The whole situation was embarrassing, and it's essentially the story of my life. I constantly discover things I should have known but didn't. For instance, I'd been working at the BYU Writing Center for more than a year when one of my fellow tutors taught me the difference between "its" and "it's." (To all the people I tutored there: It's a shame I couldn't help you with this.) I was a senior in college before I knew the word "colonel" was pronounced "kernel." And just this year I learned that tonsils aren't the thing that hangs down at the back of the throat— that's the uvula. The tonsils are the two fleshy parts on both sides of the uvula. I'm in my early 30s and I just learned that.

Like I said, it's the story of my life.

The one thing I have going for me is that I've learned to accept my condition. I'm a resigned ignoramus.

My best hope is to openly acknowledge that I have a lot to learn.

And even then the truth is hard to find.

Why the Truth Is Hard to Find

"Men occasionally stumble over the truth, but most of them pick themselves up and hurry off as if nothing ever happened." —Winston S. Churchill

The history of humanity is a lesson in the difficulty of truth finding.

Think of how long human beings thought slavery was moral, or how long we fought against the idea that the earth revolves around the sun, or how long it took for us to realize that human waste should be disposed of far from living areas rather than dumped in the streets. You'd think that last one would be the first thing humans figured out, but nope. People were still messing that up 200 to 300 years ago. We're not as smart as we sometimes think we are.

Why do we have such a hard time accepting truth in the face of compelling evidence? Here are four possibilities.

1. We feel before we reason.

"Reason is a slave to the passions." —David Hume

First we feel—*then* we reason. Not the other way around.

We were born this way.

This thought struck me after my wife and I had our first son. I used to wonder what he was thinking. Perhaps, "Why is the world so bright?" or "Why is my dad so strange looking?"

And then I realized what should have been obvious: If my son was thinking anything, he wasn't thinking in language. He was a few hours old and didn't know any words. Instead, he was 100% emotion and instinct. He felt the pangs of hunger, and he cried. He felt the comfort of being well fed, and he smiled. That was the extent of it. There was no rationality—no way for him to realize that he should stop crying and be patient because he would be fed soon. He just felt emotions and responded.

Adults often forget that at a base level, we're still wired like babies. We feel and we react. We've learned how to manage our emotions better (sometimes), but at our core, we still feel first and then reason. That is, we're prone to trust our feelings about opinions before we've vetted those opinions. In such cases, our feelings get in the way of finding the truth.

2. We prefer feelings of comfort to discomfort (and tradition brings comfort).

"A man hears what he wants to hear, and disregards the rest." —Simon & Garfunkel

If we're not careful, what we call truth is merely that which has been repeated often enough to make us feel comfortable.

This is why nearly everyone's default worldview is the one they were born into.

The French writer Michel Montaigne noted this phenomenon as he traveled across Europe. People in each country seemed to believe—without question—that they had the truth and that their customs were the best in the world. He wrote, "There is always the perfect religion, there the perfect government, there the most exact and accomplished usage of all things."

In other words, tradition blinds us with its comforts and familiarity. As the behavioral economist Daniel Kahneman once said, "Familiarity is not easily distinguished from truth."

I sometimes ask myself what my life would be like if I'd been born in another country. If I'd been born in Afghanistan or Japan, would I still be Mormon? Likely not. Instead, I would probably be a Muslim or a Buddhist.

Or say that I was born in the same place, but 500 years before. In that case, I would have been raised as part of a Native American tribe, with their traditions. As a child, I would have claimed my conviction that those traditions were true.

Chances are, you would have done the same.

Traditions are habits born before us, and habits bring us comfort.

3. We view the world from one perspective.
"The first principle is that you must not fool yourself, and you are the easiest person to fool." —Richard Feynman

No matter who we are, our first impulse is to privilege our own perspective on any given topic. This is why we immediately feel nervous when we hear an idea that conflicts with our prior beliefs. We're so close to our own way of thinking that we can't help but think we're right—even when we're wrong.

It's like how people get used to their own smell, which is why your coworker who showers only once a week has no idea that he has a problem. His nostrils are not sending the same alarms to his brain that your nostrils are sending to yours.

It's also like how most of us cringe when we hear recordings of our voices. We're surprised to discover that what we hear when we speak doesn't sound the same as what other people hear when we speak. We're always listening to our own voices through our heads, through our own perspectives.

These moments confirm that we must consult a variety of perspectives to find the truth.

4. It's really hard to rewire our perspective.

"What the human being is best at doing is interpreting all new information so that their prior conclusions remain intact." —Warren Buffett

Once we've trained our mind to think one way, it's difficult to retrain it.

To illustrate this concept, an experimenter named Destin Sandlin made a video about a bike with an inverted turning mechanism. If you turned the handlebars left, the bike went right and vice versa.

It seems like it would be simple to ride such a bike, right? Just get on, reorient your directions, and go. But it's far trickier than it sounds. Sandlin filmed random people trying to ride the bike, and no one could do it. They all got on, started to push the pedals, and immediately toppled over.

The slight tweak to the bike changed everything.

To ride the altered bike, Sandlin discovered that he had to first unlearn his automatic response to bike riding. He rode the altered bike for a few minutes a day for eight months before he could do it without difficulty.

Then when he got back on a normal bike... he couldn't ride it. At least not right away. It took him 20 minutes before the old memories clicked back into place.

By contrast, Sandlin's young son learned to ride the altered bike with relative ease. The son hadn't been riding a normal bike for long, and so it was much easier for him to learn the new process.

As with riding a bike, our biases become more and more automatic the older we get. We hear something that opposes our long-held opinions and dismiss it immediately. We don't even give it a second thought. We just *know* it's wrong.

Part of the problem is that the process of unlearning and relearning is painful and frustrating. It's like trying to ride a bike with an inverted turning mechanism. We fail again and again as we retrain our brain to think in a new way.

In a word, it's *uncomfortable*.

We Must Seek Discomfort to Find the Truth: A History of Truth Finding

To find the truth, we must occasionally let the alarms sound. We must step outside ourselves and follow reason to new, potentially frightening places. We must acknowledge that we may have picked up false beliefs—beliefs we don't realize are giving off a slight stink.

We must, above all, humbly consider that we could be wrong and talk to people who disagree with us. It will hurt in the short term, but eventually we will realize that open dialogue coupled with a dose of humility leads to a quality life.

The history of civilization proves that this is the best way forward.

The story starts like this: At the dawn of civilization, most humans were dominated by dictators—Pharaohs in Egypt, kings in Babylon, emperors in China. Power belonged to a select few, and those few often enforced their view of the truth through brutality and fear. Those who protested were slaughtered.

Then around 600 BC, something started to shift in ancient Greece.

Power began to be distributed more broadly. Democratic forms of government sprung up, most famously in Athens.

Freedom was still limited in scope, but for the first time, tens of thousands of citizens had a voice. They wrote plays that poked fun at powerful men, invented life-altering philosophies, and discovered facts about science and mathematics.

Most importantly, they realized that truth didn't always come from those with power. Instead, it could come from anyone.

The world has been indebted to ancient Greece ever since.

All was not perfect, however. Socrates once questioned his fellow citizens so thoroughly that they accused him of corrupting the youth and doubting the gods. They voted to put him to death by poison, a mandate Socrates honored even when his students, including Plato, urged him to escape. Socrates had such respect for democracy that he took the poison and died.

Time passed. Athens mishandled a series of wars, and the Roman Republic eventually occupied Greece. The Romans lifted many democratic ideals from the Greeks, but soon enough the Republic became an empire. The world reverted back to rule by domination and dictators, as seen in the rise of Julius Caesar and Caesar Augustus.

This is the world Jesus of Nazareth inhabited, and it was partly his open opposition to Roman domination that got him into trouble. The Roman Empire had little tolerance for those who overthrew tables and rebelled against authority. They crucified Jesus and killed many of his early followers.

A few hundred years later, Christians became the dominant force in Rome. They labeled their own views as orthodox (Latin for "right belief") and persecuted the heretics (Greek for "able to choose"). The followers of Jesus became the very thing he had fought against.

At this point in the narrative, Mormon missionaries tend to say that there was a falling away. They say the Great Apostasy enveloped the world in spiritual darkness for roughly 1,600 years. I taught that view of history every day while I was a Mormon missionary.

But that narrative skips right over the Islamic Golden Age.

In this era, Islamic scholars studied Greek and Roman philosophers, and in certain places, like Spain, they tolerated open discussion beyond what the world had previously seen. As a result, there was—once again—a flourishing of poetry, astronomy, mathematics, etc. Freedom of speech still had its limits, but the Islamic Golden Age was notable for its tolerance.

Thankfully, scholars in the West started to rediscover Greek and Roman philosophers, and Europeans began to doubt that truth was dictated exclusively by the Pope. With the invention of the printing press, people felt empowered to debate ideas.

Then came the Renaissance, an era of rapid discovery and disagreement. Columbus discovered America, Martin Luther posted his 95 Theses, and Shakespeare wrote subversive plays. It was another golden age.

And yet truth still struggled to gain a foothold. Radical believers continued to kill or imprison heretics such as Galileo Galilei, Giordano Bruno, and William Tyndale. Astonishingly, the Dutch philosopher Baruch Spinoza was threatened by knifepoint at a synagogue for making the now uncontroversial claim that the first five books of the Bible weren't written by Moses.

By 1644, the poet John Milton was tired of being censored by radicals. He wrote a pamphlet that declared that the best way to find truth was to let people debate. "Who ever knew truth put to the worse in a free and open encounter?" Milton asked. Then he boldly stated, "Give me the liberty to know, to utter, and to argue freely according to conscience, above all liberties."

This was the unrealized hope of democracy.

The sentiments expressed in Milton's writings paved the way for the First Amendment of the U.S. Constitution. The founders, who were also tired of being censored and vilified for their beliefs, decided that the best society was one in which everybody was free to speak their minds.

George Washington declared, "freedom of speech may be taken away—and, dumb and silent we may be led, like sheep, to the slaughter."[1] Thomas Jefferson said, "Reason and free inquiry are the only effectual agents against error."[2] And so the United States was founded as the land of the free and the home of the brave (with an embarrassing list of caveats).

Once these democratic ideals took root, the world flourished with innovation and brilliance even greater than that of ancient Athens. And after slaves were freed and women were empowered to vote, we flourished on an even greater scale.

***

Contrast the two worlds drawn above. In one world, truth was dictated by the powerful. In the other world, the one that many people inhabit today, we debate the truth without fear of being slaughtered.

Which world brings better results? Without question, the one that empowers people to debate—the one that doesn't kill people for disagreeing with what was previously considered the truth.

As societies embrace the democratic ideal with all its messiness, the lives of their citizens improve. We've seen it happen over and over again.

In my opinion, democracy is the greatest idea humanity has ever invented. It empowers us to disagree, and it's in our disagreement that we find the truth. As Joseph Smith said, "by proving contraries, truth is made manifest."[3]

Conclusion: We Must Bend Our Opinions to Fit the Truth

The trouble with truth is that it doesn't bend to fit our desired opinions.

Imagine that you traveled back in time to ancient Greece and met a man who was certain that Zeus reigned in Olympus and threw lightning from the sky. In contrast, you believe that Zeus is a myth and that lightning is caused, among other things, by positive and negative electrical charges in the clouds. Both positions can't be right, and one position has far more evidence to support it—as we can see from our vantage point in the twenty-first century.

What's interesting is that if you were to tell this ancient Greek why his position was wrong, he'd probably feel nervous, reject what you say, and keep on believing in Zeus. Why? Because all of his family and friends believe in Zeus. He trusts his family and friends. *His* family is civilized, and as a foreigner, *you're* a barbarian. So all your talk about electrical charges would just seem magical to him—or perhaps heretical—even though you're closer to the truth.

While relativity does exist (beauty is in the eye of the beholder, for instance), we do know some things with confidence. Just because an ancient Greek declared that Zeus causes lightning doesn't mean it's true for him and false for you. Instead, it's just not true. Zeus does not cause lightning.

Humanity gets closer and closer to finding the truth as we refine our thinking in light of new discoveries. We now trust satellites and scientists over oracles and shamans to predict weather patterns. We now trust vaccines over miracle healings to eliminate disease. We now wash our hands after going to the restroom instead of just returning to work. Our knowledge isn't perfect, but it has improved. It will continue to improve as we remain open to pursuing the truth wherever it leads.

There's a story I love about an elderly professor who embodied this spirit of learning. He had passionately promoted a hypothesis for a decade and a half, writing papers and making presentations that defended his position. Then one day a visiting researcher came to his university and presented convincing evidence to a crowded room that the elderly professor's long-held hypothesis was wrong. When the presentation was over, the elderly professor walked to the front, shook the visitor's hand, and said, "My dear fellow, I wish to thank you. I have been wrong these fifteen years."[4]

That's not a typical attitude toward discovering the truth, but it's the only sane way to live. Are we willing to adopt that attitude about every topic—including those that are most dear to us? If not, we'll miss out on the progress that comes from seeking the truth. As Marcus Aurelius said, "If someone is able to show me that what I think or do is not right, I will happily change, for I seek the truth, by which no one was ever truly harmed. It is the person who continues in his self-deception and ignorance who is harmed."

In the end, it comes down to two points:

1. Finding the truth isn't about being more intelligent than other people. It is about opening yourself up to the possibility of being wrong.

2. There is nothing to fear about being wrong.

Beauty, Part 2

THERE IS BEAUTY ALL AROUND

"Dwell on the beauty of life. Watch the stars, and see your self running with them."

—MARCUS AURELIUS

Beneath the Stars

It was night, and the stars were strung along the sky. I stood with the other Scouts around a campfire, watching the flames weave their way down to embers. As we stood there, our leaders gave us each a round piece of wood and asked us to think of someone we were grateful for. One by one, we named the person we'd thought of and why we were grateful for them. Then we each threw our piece of wood in the fire. Every speech was earnest and heartfelt. Many of us couldn't help but get teary eyed as we looked at the flames.

After we finished, we sang a few hymns together and ended in prayer. I then walked to a secluded place in the woods and sat alone in silence.

Somewhere in those moments beneath the stars, I felt a tremendous sense of peace. It was so powerful that it transformed my desires and made me want to be a kinder, more generous human being. In that moment, I no longer wanted to continue my long-held teenage habit of playing video games for hours each day. I wanted to live for something bigger.

It was profoundly transformative, something I wish I could experience more often.

It was a moment that happens all over the world.

***

Earlier in this book, I gave examples of beauty in the everyday sense. In this chapter, I look at beautiful moments that are more rare, profound, and even a bit mysterious. Albert Einstein said, "The most beautiful and deepest experience a man can have is the sense of the mysterious. It is the underlying principle of religion as well as all serious endeavor in art and science. He who never had this experience seems to me, if not dead, then at least blind."

My purpose here is to show that these moments are available to everyone—not just Mormons. If we can accept this idea, we will pave the way for people who disagree about belief to enjoy these experiences together. In this way we can work to save our relationships.

To demonstrate the power of these experiences, I cite dozens of stories. In this sense, I'm deliberately patterning this chapter after the work of William James, a psychologist who published a book in 1902 that documents hundreds of so-called "religious experiences"—beautiful moments of profound awe, reverence, and connection. James explains that these experiences make people happier and more generous, indicating that we should deliberately seek them out.

Experiences of Beauty in Nature

In his 1897 autobiography, *My Quest for God*, John Trevor wrote of one such experience. For a time, Trevor was away from his wife and sons, and as a result he grew depressed. Then he went on a walk in the hills with his dog.

He said, "In the loveliness of the morning, and the beauty of the hills and valleys, I soon lost my sense of sadness and regret." Then Trevor experienced something profound. He said, "On the way back, suddenly, without warning, I felt that I was in Heaven—an inward state of peace and joy and assurance indescribably intense, accompanied with a sense of being bathed in a warm glow of light, as though the external condition had brought about the internal effect—a feeling of having passed beyond the body."[1]

Trevor's words show us that these experiences are so rare and mysterious that we can't properly capture them in language. We strain for metaphor, using words like "light" and "heaven" and "a feeling of having passed beyond the body." Experiences of beauty almost demand poetic language.

Here's a similar experience from a British woman:

"In 1956 at the age of 23 my husband and I were walking the cliff path from St Ives in Cornwall to

Zennot. It was a bright sunny day in September, bright but not a garish mid-summer sun. My husband was walking his usual forty yards ahead and disappeared over the prow of an incline, so to all intents and purposes I was entirely alone. Although there was no mist, the light seemed suddenly white and diffused and I experienced the most incredible sense of oneness. ... The experience was unbelievably *beautiful*."[2]

Importantly, these experiences aren't limited to people who believe in God. To illustrate, the atheist Andre Comte-Sponville had a comparable experience as a young man. "The first time it happened, I was in a forest in the north of France," he says. "I must have been twenty-five or twenty-six. ... That particular evening, some friends and I had gone out for a walk in the forest we liked so much. Night had fallen. We were walking. Gradually our laughter faded, and the conversation died down. Nothing remained but our friendship, our mutual trust and shared presence. ... I was simply registering the world around me—the darkness of the underbrush, the incredible luminosity of the sky, the faint sounds of the forest (branches snapping, an occasional animal call, our own muffled steps) only making the silence more palpable. And then, all of a sudden... What? Nothing: everything! No words, no meanings, no questions, only—a surprise. Only—this. A seemingly infinite happiness. A seemingly eternal sense of peace. Above me, the starry sky was immense, luminous and unfathomable, and within me there was nothing but the sky, of which I was a part, and the silence, and the light, like a warm hum, and a sense of joy. ... Yes, in the darkness of that night, I contained only the dazzling presence of the All. Peace. Infinite peace! Simplicity, serenity, delight."[3]

Comte-Sponville describes his experience as momentarily inhabiting "the oceanic feeling"—a feeling so grand that those who experience it say they are at one with the universe.

Comte-Sponville then cites other atheists who have had similarly profound spiritual experiences. One of them said, "The border between my body and the world had vanished. ... Everything was there, more present than ever before." Another said that the experience felt like "eternity now. Immortal life now." Another said, "I saw nothing that was new, but I saw all the usual things in a new and miraculous light—in what I believe to be their true light. ... I saw that this beauty was everywhere present."

Again, these accounts are from people who were atheists before they had these experiences and who remained atheists afterward. This calls into question William James's use of the term "religious experience." In reality, these experiences are available to all of humanity, regardless of our beliefs.

By this point, we can notice a few patterns that lead to these experiences of beauty: 1) walking in nature 2) talking with a friend 3) silence.

The talk show host Oprah Winfrey once shared a story that follows this pattern. She's about as different from Comte-Sponville as a person can get, but I'm struck by how similar their stories are. They live thousands of miles apart, and yet they both had essentially the same powerful experience in nature.

Winfrey says, "My friend Bob Greene and I were taking a hike. The sun had set, leaving wisps of lavender ribbons across the sky. Clouds moving down from the mountain spread out over the ocean, with only a small opening through which we could see the moon...

"As we continued our walk, Bob turned to me and said, 'Stop a minute.'

"I stopped.

"'Can you hear that?' he whispered.

"I could—and it took my breath away. 'It' was the sound of silence. Utter and complete stillness. So still I could hear my own heart beating. I wanted to hold my breath, because even inhaling and exhaling was like a cacophony. There was absolutely no movement, no breeze, no recognition of air, even; it was the sound of nothing and everything. It felt like all life...and death...and beyond contained in one space, and I was not just standing in it, I was also a part of 'it.' This was the most peaceful, coherent, knowledgeable moment I've ever witnessed."[4]

Beauty in Music

Of course, beautiful experiences don't happen exclusively in nature. They also happen through artistic expression, perhaps especially through music.

The business tycoon J.C. Penney once told a story that illustrates this point. In 1929, he was hospitalized because of severe anxiety. One night he grew so sick that he wrote farewell letters to his wife and son. He was certain he was going to die.

However, he survived the night and woke the next morning to hear singing in the nearby hospital chapel. He walked in and listened. Then he said, "Suddenly something happened. I can't explain it. I can only call it a miracle. I felt as if I had been instantly lifted out of the darkness of a dungeon into warm brilliant sunlight. I felt as if I had been transported from hell to paradise. ... From that day to this, my life has been free from worry. I am 71 years old, and the most dramatic and glorious 20 minutes of my life were those I spent in that chapel that morning."[5]

Here's another experience, this one of a man listening to music. "I was sitting one evening, listening to a Brahms symphony," he said. "My eyes were closed and I must have been completely relaxed for I became aware of a feeling of 'expansion,' I seemed to be beyond the boundary of my physical self. Then an intense feeling of 'light' and 'love' uplifted and enfolded me. It was so wonderful and gave me such an emotional release that tears streamed down my cheeks. For several days I seemed to bathe in its glow and when it subsided I was free from my fears. ... I can truly say that it changed my life and the subsequent years have brought no dimming of the experience."[6]

In an interview with Charlie Rose, the songwriter Paul Simon talked about how he sometimes experiences profound beauty when he writes music. Simon illustrates the mystery of a beautiful experience. He says, "You never know when you're going to feel it. In my experience it's not a common occurrence, but there have been times when I've written a line that I had no idea I was about to write that just made me stop and lose my breath or cry. And I didn't know why, and I don't mean to say this as if I'm bragging about how good it was because most of the time I really thought, 'how did that happen?'

"The first time that I can remember it was when I wrote 'Bridge Over Troubled Water' — not the whole song, but just the melody line: 'Like a bridge over troubled water I will lay me down.' One second it didn't exist. The next six seconds it was there. And I was just shocked. I thought, 'that's so much better than I usually write. I wonder where that came from.' Of course I was 27 or 28, so I hadn't really thought about how sometimes you get plugged into a big, big force and you're a conduit—that's how it feels like. It's nothing to brag about; it's something to be grateful for."

Rose: "You feel that? That there's some bigger force and you take it when it comes and celebrate the fact that it gave you the power to do what you just did?"

Simon: "Yes, I do, but I don't want to go into the next step and say that I think that bigger force is God. Nor do I want to say it's not. But I do want to recognize that there are times when something comes to you and you don't know why, and there it is and you feel very satisfied. You get this feeling that's very close to bliss."[7]

Beauty as Oneness

Almost all the experiences I've shared so far occurred in solitude, but solitude is not a prerequisite. These moments can also occur in energetic crowds, when you feel unified with everyone present.

Tony Hsieh, CEO of the shoe company Zappos, once described experiencing deep spiritual connection at a party in a warehouse the size of ten football fields. The place was packed with people dancing to the beat of electronic music. Fog machines and laser beams created a surreal atmosphere. Hsieh was struck by how earnestly the dancers were trying to feel the music rather than impress their friends. Something about the sincerity and energy of the scene struck a chord in him. He said, "I was surprised to feel myself swept with an overwhelming sense of spirituality— not in the religious sense, but a sense of deep connection with everyone who was there as well as the rest of the universe."[8]

One man described feeling something similar at a sporting event. He said, "I was at a football game in the Astrodome, waiting in the concession line. All at once, I felt as if I were inside the minds of all the people around me and that I could feel what they were feeling. I could feel their happiness, their love for their friends and family, and their joy at being together. Though it only lasted for a few moments, it was like tapping into the Spirit of God."[9]

I felt this way one night as a participant at Especially for Youth (EFY). Everyone had gathered together in a packed auditorium on BYU campus. There we sang a medley of "As Sisters in Zion" and

"The Army of Helaman." We sang with such conviction and earnestness that in the middle of the song I was struck with a magnificent feeling of unity with everyone in the room and even beyond the room.

Beauty is the experience of feeling at one.

The neuroscientist Jill Bolte Taylor felt this unity one day when she woke up and experienced the symptoms of a stroke. Midway through the experience, she felt something transcendent. She said, "I was immediately captivated by the magnificence of the energy around me. And because I could no longer identify the boundaries of my body, I felt enormous and expansive. I felt at one with all the energy that was, and it was beautiful there."[10]

The astronaut Edgar Mitchell had a comparable experience as he looked at Earth from space. He said, "What I experienced during that three-day trip home was nothing short of an overwhelming sense of universal connectedness. ... I perceived the universe as in some way conscious."[11]

***

Thankfully, we don't need to have a stroke or go to space to access this feeling of beauty and universal connection.

Instead we can deliberately choose activities that will increase the chances that we'll encounter profound beauty. As this chapter shows, we can spend more time in nature, enjoy the presence of friends, listen to powerful music, and be fully present in energetic crowds.

The more time we spend participating in these activities instead of pursuing mindless distractions, the greater the chance that we'll experience the mysterious.

We can experience these profound moments of beauty together despite our differences of belief. As professor of theology Paul Badham said, "Dogmas divide, experience unites."[12] These experiences of profound beauty are critical to saving our relationships. They're an essential component of a quality life.

Goodness, Part 2

GOOD GUYS VERSUS BAD GUYS

"I never considered a difference of opinion in politics, in religion, in philosophy as cause for withdrawing from a friend."
—THOMAS JEFFERSON

Binary Thinking
"Does it have bad guys in it?"

That's the question my four-year-old son would ask me whenever I suggested a show to watch. Often my answer was no, there were no bad guys in it. The shows I suggested (*Blue's Clues, Kipper the Dog, Mister Rogers' Neighborhood,* etc.) featured characters that simply talked about ideas or solved puzzles. No bad guys.

When I tried to explain that shows with no bad guys were fun, my son would complain. "So boring!" he would say (even though he liked those shows when he watched them).

"Why does a show need to have bad guys in it?" I once asked him.

"Because I like seeing them defeated," he said.

I wonder how often we all have that desire. Do we crave separating people into groups of good guys and bad guys? Do we crave seeing our opponents defeated?

As I've witnessed debates about Mormonism over the years, I get the sense that the answer is yes. I've seen believing Mormons label those who leave as wayward apostates, as projects in desperate need of reconversion. I've seen former Mormons label those who stay as blind followers, as sheep trundling down a path rife with subtle intolerance. To each way of thinking, the wayward and the intolerant are the "bad guys."

I've wrestled with these tensions myself. Before I learned how messy Church history is, I thought everyone who doubted was misguided. I felt sorry for them and proud that I was still on course for the many blessings that await the righteous.

Now that I've learned a few uncomfortable things about Church history, I sometimes feel superior to people who are less informed on the topic. I find myself looking down on people who say incorrect things about the Church—things I would have said just a few years ago.

When I catch myself in these unkind moments, I'm disgusted. What's wrong with me? How can I think such mean-spirited thoughts when there is still so much I don't know?

What's wrong with me is that, like most people, I struggle to think outside of my own ideology. I struggle to think beyond binaries.

Beyond Binaries

Jonathan Haidt, a professor of psychology at New York University, experienced this struggle with binary thinking too. He was raised as a liberal atheist, and in college he was an open critic of Ronald Reagan, certain in his belief that the religious right essentially consisted of immoral rednecks. He openly advocated for secular liberal causes.

But before graduation, Haidt traveled to India. There he interviewed people who had tremendous respect for tradition and authority. They embraced many of the conservative values he had rejected his whole life. For the first time, Haidt realized that conservative values had merit. They brought a level of stability, safety, and community that he hadn't yet experienced in his own life.

When he returned to the United States and became a full-fledged professor, he started interviewing people outside his ideological peer group. He talked to conservatives in rural communities, people whose views he'd never seriously considered before.

After compiling thousands of data points from his interviews and surveys, he realized that liberals and conservatives both want to improve the world, but they approach the task with different primary values. Whereas liberals primarily value caring for the vulnerable, conservatives primarily value preserving community.

Haidt also observed that liberals had moral failings he hadn't recognized before. In one study, he asked thousands of conservatives and liberals to complete a survey about their moral beliefs. Afterward, he asked them to fill out the same survey but from the viewpoint of their ideological opponents. Conservatives accurately defined what liberals believe, but liberals were way off in defining the beliefs of conservatives (as defined by conservatives). In other words, liberals struggled to understand their ideological opponents in a way that conservatives didn't.

As part of his studies, Haidt also discovered benefits to religion. He found that religiously observant Americans give more time and money to their ingroup *and* to outside secular causes than nonbelievers do. In addition, he found that religious communities are far more likely than secular communities to remain intact over decades. This stability creates stronger communities and relationships—a key component to a quality life.

As a result of his studies, Jonathan Haidt did something remarkable.

He changed his mind.

He no longer viewed all conservatives as bad guys. He was still a liberal atheist, but he could now see that the world consists of human beings who are all struggling to do their best. He saw that it was possible to disagree with someone else's position and still see them as fully human rather than as evil incarnate. He saw that religious conservatives had qualities he wanted to integrate into his own life. He dropped the binary of good guys versus bad guys.[1]

In the same vein as Haidt, the economist Arnold Kling has invented a framework that can help us drop false binaries and make more sense of the state of contemporary Mormon culture.[2]

Kling talks about three major ideological languages, each primarily concerned with achieving a different end.

Here's roughly how he outlines these ideologies and their differences:

Conservatives are primarily concerned with preserving order and avoiding chaos.
Progressives are primarily concerned with pursuing equality and avoiding oppression.
Libertarians are primarily concerned with promoting freedom and avoiding coercion.

It's a simple framework that can help us work through our ideological confrontations.

First, we can frame an issue as our opponents frame it. This is the first step to resolving conflict. For example, if progressives frame a position as a struggle between order and chaos, they'll have more productive conversations with conservatives. The two groups will be speaking the same ideological language, and they will better understand each other. From there, they can discuss other ways to look at the position, including how it affects equality. This process can help in any ideological confrontation.

Second, we can reject the notion that we must identify strictly as conservative, progressive, or libertarian. We can accept that there is a time to preserve order, a time to pursue equality, and a time to promote freedom. We can fight for the right cause at the right time without always identifying with one ideology. We can realize that what is good depends on the context. To everything there is a season.

Third, we can discover our commonalities. For instance, it's possible to frame an issue as promoting order, equality, *and* freedom. Once an issue is framed in all three ideological languages, a majority may start to support it. In this way, people with different core ideologies can move forward together.

This framework can also help us better understand the strengths and weaknesses of mainstream Mormon ideology. With this understanding, we'll be less likely to look down on people who do or do not fit a certain mold. Instead we'll see them as human beings who are navigating complicated choices and trying to do their best.

Mormons in the Beehive

It's no secret that of the three ideological languages, contemporary Mormonism aligns most closely with conservatism. In fact, the Pew Research Center has found that no religious group in the United States favors conservative ideology more than the Mormons.[3]

There are times when equality and freedom get mentioned in church manuals, and there are many members who aren't conservative. But the constant refrain in most church meetings is order. Keep the commandments. Heed the words of the prophets. Have a current temple recommend. Follow the law of tithing and the law of chastity. Live the Word of Wisdom. Attend your ward meetings. Read the standard works. Attend the temple regularly.

To critics of the Church, such rules might seem like the opposite of goodness. These critics say that the never-ending reminders to follow the rules cause Mormons to worry about the letter of the law instead of the spirit. They might say that the Church has wandered from the Sacred Grove and is stuck in the beehive.

There's validity to that position, but I think many of these critics might underestimate how wonderful order can be. In the case of Mormonism, order enables church members to go almost anywhere in the world and find friends who have the same values they do. Order creates community, and many people find strength in community.

In fact, when a group of unorthodox Mormons were asked why they stay in the Church, they claimed that the main reason was community. Here's a sample of what they said.

1. "Why do I stay? For me, I feel invested, and Mormonism is my tribe."
2. "My heritage and family. They are such genuinely good people, and I don't want to lose them."
3. "Community."
4. "I ask myself that question fairly often. Probably mostly social. I like being part of a spiritual community."
5. "My friends. Not wanting to disappoint my ancestors."
6. "Communion."

7. "For better and for worse, I'm a Mormon. It's just who I am."
8. "My husband."
9. "My relationships with friends at church."
10. "There is goodness. Maybe more or less than other communities and people, but there is palpable goodness. Although I see many things much differently, I still find the good."

These people recognize the value of a well-ordered community. They recognize that as much as certain aspects of Mormonism trouble them, they can appreciate the sociality the religion brings. I admire those who can see that the order within Mormonism carries many upsides.

And yet despite all this, the pursuit of order carries many downsides as well. It can cause members to ignore people who don't fit a certain mold, to follow tradition for tradition's sake, and to live contrary to their inner voice. It can confuse people into thinking that obedience to a hierarchy is the only way to be moral, or even the best way to be moral. In Mormonism, the pursuit of order has caused members to adopt bad traditions (such as denying blacks the priesthood) and then hold onto those traditions for far too long. Finally, the pursuit of order has brought a tendency to conflate faithful church membership with the Republican Party in the United States. This conflation of religious and political identity alienates Mormons who don't identify with Republican ideals. It also causes conservative Mormons to support politicians whose ethics they wouldn't otherwise support.

Of course, the other ideologies also have downsides.

Progressive ideology sometimes disregards traditional values without seeing how traditions tie communities together. In fact, sometimes progressives believe there isn't a single tradeoff to breaking from tradition. This equates to liberal smugness, an attitude illustrated in Jonathan Haidt's study wherein liberals failed to articulate what conservatives actually believe. Liberals also occasionally enable governments to constrain freedom in the name of helping the common wage earner. Without proper constraints, this moral strong-arming can devolve into authoritarianism, as we've seen in communist governments across the globe.

In a similar vein, the pursuit of freedom sometimes leads libertarians to continually pull up institutions by the roots, creating unending instability. Think of the bloody mess of the French Revolution, an era where people struggled to find a foothold and gain some semblance of order. The pursuit of freedom also sometimes harms minorities, who often have no recourse except to appeal to the authority of the government when their rights are trampled. In this way, even the pursuit of freedom can carry negative consequences.

However, even when an ideology reaches its limits, it doesn't mean that those who subscribe to that ideology are morally bankrupt. It just means that they've become so blinded by their pursuit of a good thing that they can't discern the flaws. They feel as though their moral standards override everyone else's.

They're wrong to feel this way, and they can only right this wrong by stepping back, looking more objectively at the situation, and admitting that every ideology has upsides and downsides.

Goodness in Context

Once we see that every ideology has upsides and downsides, we can start to respect a plurality of beliefs. We can also see, as I mentioned above, that we must choose the right stance in the right situation instead of blindly sticking to a single ideology at all costs.

Since this point can help us save our relationships when we disagree ideologically, let's look at two examples of how it works. First, we'll look at the history of the United States. Then we'll look at the history of Mormonism. Both show that the morality of an ideology depends on the context.

The United States has privileged freedom, order, and equality at various times. The seeds of the nation were planted with the libertarian impulse to reject the coercive rule of a distant government. The founders fought for freedom even at the risk of death. Freedom was their primary concern.

Shortly after winning that freedom, however, many founders were cautious of the chaos that comes with a revolutionary mindset. This group included Alexander Hamilton and John Adams, men who knew that the nation needed order to survive. They said the best way to maintain order was to uphold the tradition of a powerful centralized government. Thankfully, other founders such as Thomas Jefferson balanced out the demands for centralized power, and the young nation ended up with a relatively healthy blend of order and freedom.

However, the debate about order versus freedom didn't do much to help oppressed minorities. As a result, the nation soon wrestled to find the right blend of order and equality. Heroes such as Abraham Lincoln, Susan B. Anthony, and Martin Luther King Jr. now receive almost universal praise for their progressive efforts on this front.

I can't claim to know which of these three ideological languages (if any) is best given today's complicated political climate. I will only say that the history of the United States shows that no single ideological language is inherently right or wrong. It shows that heroes can rise from any ideological framework.

Mormonism has also privileged different ideological languages at different times.

The religion started with the progressive and libertarian ideals of Joseph Smith, whose visionary worldview broke sharply from traditional religion and even from oppressive state governments. He published new scripture, started new rituals, spoke against political coercion, and boldly proclaimed that we should have all things in common.

But all that energy needed organization when Smith died. This is where Brigham Young's skills became valuable. Young organized the Saints and led them West—a trek that benefited from Young's insistence on order. The early Saints needed order to survive the plains and settle the rugged Utah landscape. Young excelled at this, as bullheaded as he sometimes was.

Ever since Brigham Young, however, Mormonism has doubled down on order—creating unified lesson manuals, worldwide standards of worthiness, and hierarchical structures across the Church. We've seen the upsides of order in a heightened sense of community. We've also seen the downsides, where those who don't fit a certain mold feel anxiety and spiritual pain within the religion.

To find goodness, we must find the right blend of order, equality, and freedom. For my part, I believe that orthodox Mormons would benefit by holding less tightly to order, while unorthodox Mormons would benefit by holding more tightly to it.

Love Is the Only Option

Above all, we must see that people aren't corrupt just because their beliefs differ from our own. We must recognize that the world isn't a melodrama, made up of bad guys and good guys. Instead, the world consists of people with divergent motives and viewpoints.

It's true that sometimes our views of goodness are irreconcilable. In these instances, there is power in realizing that two opposing beliefs might be just the thing the world needs to move forward. We don't always need to convert someone else to our way of thinking to make the world a better place. We can accept that two opposing opinions could both be right in different ways and to different degrees.

Goodness is often found in the dialogue between opposing viewpoints.

If we can recognize this, we can save our relationships even when we disagree. We can recognize that the world consists of flawed human beings generally trying to do their very best.

Truth, Part 2

THE QUESTING SPIRIT

"I admire men and women who have developed the questing spirit; who are unafraid of new ideas as stepping stones to progress."
—HUGH B. BROWN

Wrong Again

I was two weeks into my mission when I got into my first debate about Church history.

My companion and I knocked on the door of a guy who turned out to be a religious history buff. He invited us in to talk. Throughout our discussion, he kept insisting that Joseph Smith had a gun and shot people in Carthage Jail.

Being the naive missionary I was, I told him he was wrong. As proof, I showed him the official account of Smith's martyrdom in the Doctrine and Covenants. The account mentions nothing about Smith shooting anyone, much less anything about a gun.

Unfortunately for us, the guy wasn't persuaded by this account, and we left without getting him to commit to pray about whether Joseph Smith was a prophet.

A few months later, I was digging around a library in an LDS Church building and found *A Comprehensive History of the Church* by B. H. Roberts, a Mormon General Authority. There I discovered that Smith had indeed shot people in Carthage Jail.

Now, in the grand scheme of things, the fact that Joseph Smith shot some people wasn't earth shattering. It was the Wild West, and he was scared for his life. I would have wanted to have a gun in Carthage Jail too.

And yet this discovery troubled me.

Years earlier, I had watched an official seminary video about Joseph Smith's martyrdom that was so moving it nearly brought me to tears. The scene was riveting, and Smith seemed so noble that the film served as a foundational building block in my testimony of the prophet.

However, in this official video, Smith had no gun. He didn't shoot anyone. He was defenseless when he was murdered.

As I reflected about the discrepancy between that seminary video and what I had just discovered in a church library, I felt deceived. Someone had whitewashed an official church video to make the story more inspirational. That is, they had privileged beauty over truth rather than seeking for the proper blend of both.

This realization didn't lead me to any drastic conclusions about the validity of the Church, but it did force me to ask what other truths I didn't know about Mormon history. It put me in a position where I was willing to question.

***

Another surprise for me came one summer night on my mission when my companion and I passed by an open window. From inside we heard a group of college students making jokes about Mormons. We stopped and listened for a while and then, like any good missionaries, we knocked on the door.

The college students were wide-eyed and speechless when they answered. They invited us in, trying to stifle laughs, and said that they'd recently watched an episode of *South Park* that was all about the Mormons.

They asked us how much of the episode was true.

Specifically, they were wondering whether Joseph Smith really looked into a hat to translate the Book of Mormon.

This was the first time I had ever heard of such a thing. I told them that of course it wasn't true, and that you couldn't believe everything you saw on a cartoon like *South Park*. Instead, I explained, Joseph Smith translated the Book of Mormon from a set of gold plates under the direction of God.

They listened politely and then denied our request to take the missionary discussions. We left feeling good that we had helped set the record straight in some small way.

But we hadn't set the record straight. We had just repeated what we had been taught in Sunday School. I later learned from official Church sources that, yes, Joseph Smith did use a hat to translate the Book of Mormon. I felt embarrassed that I first learned this fact from a bunch of college students who'd seen a cartoon on Comedy Central.

Questions Bring Pain, Then Growth
"The truth will set you free, but first it will make you miserable." —Jamie Buckingham

Both of these experiences on my mission caused me to ask questions about the Church. Ultimately, these questions have improved my life, even though they were deeply uncomfortable at the time. As Dieter F. Uchtdorf says, "I'm not sure how one can discover truth without asking questions. ... Asking questions isn't a sign of weakness. It's a precursor to growth."

In this chapter, I delve into uncomfortable questions about Mormon history. I'm not the first to do this, and I recognize that these questions will potentially inspire doubt. The goal of this section, and of this entire book, is not to launch faithful members of the Church into open water without a lifeline. That said, the quest for truth requires us to face difficult facts.

Talking openly about these facts is the only way to bridge differences between those who believe and those who doubt. We can't just agree to unite around flawed narratives and sweep our discomfort aside. No matter how strong our convictions, we can't vote on history. We can't say, "Let's agree that Joseph Smith didn't have a gun in Carthage Jail and that he didn't look into a hat to translate the Book of Mormon." Instead, we must be willing to accept events in Mormon history as they really happened—especially when official LDS sources acknowledge their truthfulness. Healthy spiritual progress and healthy relationships aren't afraid of the truth.

The Church is increasingly open about uncomfortable facts. As I mentioned in the introduction, they've published a series of essays on LDS.org that openly address uncomfortable moments in Church history.[1] Topics include the translation of the Book of Abraham, polygamy after 1890, the multiple accounts of the First Vision, the ban on blacks holding the priesthood, the Mountain Meadows Massacre, and more. These Church-approved essays are a move in the right direction. They're paving the way for members to have an open dialogue without the fear of being labeled as wayward for their doubts.

Stories of Doubt

"The honest investigator must be prepared to follow wherever the search of truth may lead." —Hugh B. Brown

To illustrate why some people struggle to believe in Mormonism, I've listed three stories below. None of the stories prove that the Church is true or false, nor do they indicate that anyone should stop belonging to the Church. In reality, there are many people who happily remain Mormon even though they know every fact mentioned in this chapter and more. If you're interested, you can see the endnotes for a list of faith-affirming resources on these topics.[2]

Put simply, these three stories illustrate why we should feel empathy for people on both sides of the discussion. Each story is based on a collection of real experiences.

1. Maren and Ryan

Maren and Ryan are a married couple with two young girls. Maren has been raised with the belief that men and women are equally valuable to God. Maren sometimes struggles to believe this about herself, but overall she feels confident of God's love. She and Ryan live their lives in harmony with the teachings of Mormonism.

One day Maren is on the Church's family history site when she discovers that Joseph Smith had 34 wives—some already married, some very young. She sees that Smith married Helen Kimball when he was 37 and she was 14.

She also finds that the prophets following Smith married teenage girls as well. For instance, she sees that Lorenzo Snow married a 15-year-old girl when he was 57. Then she sees that Snow had five children with her, the last of which was born when he was 82 years old.

Something about this doesn't feel right to Maren, and it makes her so depressed that she can't read further. She continues to go to church, say her prayers, and read her scriptures, hoping that her depression will just go away. But one night she reads some verses in Doctrine & Covenants 132 that say, "if [a man] have ten virgins given unto him by this law, he cannot commit adultery, for they belong to him ... But if one or either of the ten virgins, after she is espoused, shall be with another man, she has committed adultery, and shall be destroyed; for they are given unto him..." These verses make her feel awful inside. She wonders how a God who loves her could talk about women being "given unto" men. To Maren, that's how someone might talk about a cow. As property.

Now she doesn't know what to believe. She questions how she can reconcile her love of Mormonism with her disgust for polygamy.

When she brings up what she has found to her husband, Ryan, he tells her not to look at that stuff. She says that she found the information on the Church's own sites and in scripture, but Ryan tells her that she needs to just stick to reading about the gospel. He says she needs to recognize that God sometimes requires us to accept hard things as a test of our faith, and it will all make sense in the afterlife. He asks her not to bring it up again.

Later, as Ryan reflects on his conversation with his wife, he thinks about two conflicting feelings: 1) the dark feeling he had while talking to Maren about polygamy and 2) the beautiful feeling he had while praying on his mission to know if the Book of Mormon were true.

He tells himself that while he doesn't understand the reasons for polygamy, he should trust the feeling of peace from his mission as proof that this is God's work. He resolves that he will tell his wife he loves her more often.

Maren, for her part, wonders what she should teach her daughters.

2. David and Brother Williams

David, a BYU student, gets an assignment in his religion class from his professor, Brother Williams, to write a paper about the Book of Mormon.

To start his research, David visits the BYU library and comes across *Studies of the Book of Mormon*, a book by LDS Apostle B. H. Roberts. In the book, Roberts presents various explanations for how the Book of Mormon came to be. One section addresses Joseph Smith's imaginative capacities. Here Roberts claims that "there can be no question" that Joseph Smith was "possessed of a sufficiently vivid and creative imagination as to produce such a work as the Book Mormon."

David reads the range of evidence Roberts uses to support his claim. This evidence includes the testimony of Joseph Smith's mother, Lucy, who said that, starting at the age of 18, Joseph told stories about the ancient Americans "with as much ease, seemingly, as if he had spent his whole life among them."

Roberts asserts that because Joseph Smith started telling these stories many years before he received the gold plates, "these evening recitals could come from no other source than the vivid, constructive imagination of Joseph Smith." Roberts adds that this was "a remarkable power which attended [Smith] through all his life." He then says that the power "was as strong and varied as Shakespeare's and no more to be accounted for than the English Bard's."

These words from B. H. Roberts disorient David completely. Before that moment, David had never considered it possible that Joseph Smith could have created the Book of Mormon from his imagination. And yet here was an LDS Apostle claiming as much.

Compelled by his curiosity, David types "Did Joseph Smith write the Book of Mormon?" into Google. He reads theories about how Smith reapplied ideas and phrases from books such as the Bible, *View of the Hebrews*, *The First Book of Napoleon*, and *The Late War*. He reads about anachronisms, DNA analysis, and changes that have been made to the text.[3]

David feels overwhelmed by all this information and doesn't know what to do. Above all, he hopes the most troubling claims aren't true.

Feeling desperate, the next day he decides to bring up his concerns to his religion professor, Brother Williams.

Brother Williams tells David that he can find some answers on FairMormon.org, but that ultimately it's most important to listen to the whisperings of the Spirit and not to lose sight of the blessings that the Church brings to people's lives. David thinks about pressing Brother Williams further, but he worries that his questions may affect his grade. He thanks Brother Williams for his time and goes home.

After class, Brother Williams sits in his office feeling anxious about the questions David raised. He thinks of his sister who left the Church over questions similar to David's and how sad she seems to him now. Her husband divorced her when she told him she no longer believed, and she hasn't been nearly as close to her own parents and siblings ever since. He knows he doesn't have all the answers, but also knows that the Church has brought endless blessings into his life. He prays to feel the love of God and a reassurance that he is doing what is right.

Back in his apartment, David spends the night researching his questions on FairMormon.org. Some of the explanations make sense to him, but mostly the site just confirms that the truth is more complex than he had previously thought.

3. Janice & Becky

Janice, a Relief Society president with a gay teenage son named Josh, has struggled to know how to handle the Church's policies on homosexuality. The more she studies about the topic and the more she listens to Josh explain himself, the more convinced she becomes that homosexuality is tied to biology and, especially in the case of her son, isn't about sin and rebellion. She also feels uneasy about the idea that Josh will either have to end up in an unfulfilling heterosexual relationship or will have to leave the Church to find someone to love.

When Janice first learns of the Church's policy that children of homosexuals can't be baptized, she is stunned. It's one thing for the Church to not allow gay marriage. It's another thing entirely to exclude children from baptism. To Janice, children are innocent, and none of the official explanations about why they should be excluded from baptism feel right to her. The policy isn't consistent with her understanding of love or compassion.

All this internal wrestling leads Janice to consider that the Church may have been misguided on this topic. At the very least, she hopes that the Church might change its position in some way. To find hope, she studies similar examples from the past and finds that whereas the Church once discouraged marriage between blacks and whites, they no longer have any problem with it. She finds that Brigham Young once said, "Shall I tell you the law of God in regard to the African race? If the white man who belongs to the chosen seed mixes his blood with the seed of Cain, the penalty, under the law of God, is death on the spot." And then, just for good measure, he added, "This will always be so." While this quote lowers Janice's estimation of Brigham Young, it gives her hope that the Church will change as it develops a greater understanding of homosexuality.

Janice also finds that while prior church leaders had publicly spoken out against birth control, the theory of evolution, blacks having the priesthood, sex education in public schools, and the United States (for kicking Mormons out of Illinois)[4], they no longer do. Again, this gives her hope that they might change their stance on homosexuality as well.

One night Janice lets slip to her family that she thinks it's possible that the Church is wrong for banning the children of homosexuals from baptism. As soon as she says this, her oldest daughter, Becky, who is married and has one child, becomes upset and says that her own mom—a Relief Society president, no less—should know better than to question the Brethren.

At this, Josh stands up and quietly leaves the table, and the rest of the family feels a tension they haven't felt in years.

To break the silence, Becky tells her family that she loves them. She says that blessings come from following the prophets and that the prophets won't lead the Church astray.

Janice says she doesn't know what she believes, and she walks upstairs to comfort Josh.

Through Sorrow to Joy

"For in much wisdom is much grief: and he that increaseth knowledge increaseth sorrow." —Ecclesiastes

As I've written them here, these stories all end in sorrow.

Scenes like these occur in homes, churches, and institute classrooms all over. They're scenes of heartbreak, familial tension, and spiritual loneliness.

But what happens after each scene?

We're the ones who determine that. These are the stories we're living within the contemporary Mormon community, and we have the power to choose where the stories go, how they really end.

If we think through the possible outcomes, we can see a range of options.

Option #1: We can ignore anything that makes us uncomfortable.

This option is unsustainable in the Internet age, where evidence about Mormon history is easier than ever to find. The ease of access is not going away, and those who ignore history will discover that not all their family members and friends will get in line—especially since many uncomfortable facts are now easily accessible on LDS.org. In other words, the choice to ignore anything that brings discomfort will certainly end in sorrow as we ignore the legitimate concerns of the people we love.

Option #2: We can look at the evidence and feel smug about what we've found.

Some of us have felt judgmental and mean-spirited toward those who don't know certain facts about Mormon history—facts we may have only recently discovered ourselves. But feeling smug only widens the divide between friends and family, causing our story to end in sorrow. In a world with endless knowledge, there's no room to feel smug about something we've learned. There is only room to feel humility about all the things we have yet to learn.

Option #3: We can look at the evidence and commit to a balanced pursuit of truth, beauty, and goodness.

Henry Eyring, the famous Mormon chemist, once told his son Henry B. Eyring that "in this church you don't have to believe anything that isn't true." I'd like to take Henry Eyring at his word. I don't have to believe anything that isn't true. I also don't have to go to endless lengths to rationalize a truth claim, especially if I wouldn't rationalize a similar truth claim from another religion. I can just accept that the particular truth claim isn't valid.

Richard Bushman, a Mormon patriarch and historian whose works are promoted at Deseret Book, stated the situation bluntly. He said, "I think that for the Church to remain strong it has to reconstruct its narrative. The dominant narrative is not true. It can't be sustained. The Church has to absorb all this new information, or it will be on very shaky grounds. That's what it is trying to do and it will be a strain for a lot of people, older people especially. But I think it has to change." It's important to note that Bushman isn't saying that all faith-affirming narratives are false. For instance, he still believes in the divine origin of Mormonism and that Joseph Smith was inspired.[5] However, he is saying that the Church has to adjust its narrative in light of the historical facts. And that might be hard for some people.

As I've mentioned, the truth doesn't always lead to instant joy. Often it makes us miserable at first. We realize that there are no perfect answers, and we have to learn how to be comfortable with uncertainty and doubt.

However, when we couple the pursuit of truth with the appropriate measure of beauty and goodness, we find that the truth is far more bearable. Given time, we will find that our joy has deepened as a result of our knowledge. We've passed through sorrow to joy, and we realize we would never trade truth for ignorance.

My hope for the people in these stories—Maren and Ryan, David and Brother Williams, Janice and Becky—is that they can unite around truth, beauty, and goodness. My hope is that they be forgiving and compassionate as they learn and re-adjust together. If people on both sides can acknowledge the truth and do so with love and kindness, our stories will end happily. The truth will set us free.

For part three, I start with goodness because the chapter elaborates on Richard Bushman's testimony.

Goodness, Part 3

PURE RELIGION

"Religion that is pure and undefiled before God, the Father, is this: to visit orphans and widows in their affliction, and to keep oneself unstained from the world."

—JAMES 1:27

Mormonism Is the Ward

One hot and humid day when he was bishop, Harvard professor Clayton Christensen visited an elderly woman in his ward.

The moment he entered her house he was overwhelmed with a horrible stench. Several grapefruit had been forgotten in a defunct iron fridge, and they were now rotting and swelling in the basement. Since the woman had lost her sense of smell, she was unaware of how repugnant her living quarters had become.

Christensen phoned a nearby non-Mormon friend for help, and together they heaved the fridge up the stairs to get it out of the house.

As they paused on a step, sweaty and struggling under the smell, the friend mentioned that he didn't know much about Mormonism. Christensen caught his breath and thought about how he could explain the religion to his friend.

Instead of explaining the doctrine, he looked at the scene and said, "This is about it."

When Christensen later recounted this story to a group of journalists, he said that the point was simply that "if you want to understand Mormonism, you have to understand the ward."

I can sympathize with Christensen's point. If you're an active Mormon, your main religious concern likely centers on fulfilling your ward calling. This is what day-to-day Mormonism means to most members, and it all has to do with the ward.

Because of the ward, my family was aware of the elderly in our neighborhood and would visit them on Sunday afternoons. Because of the ward, we knew who was struggling financially, and we could rally to help them during the holidays. Because of the ward, I interacted on a personal level with a range of generous adults (Scout leaders, bishops, teachers, etc.) who I wouldn't have known otherwise.

Importantly, it's not that people who don't belong to a ward don't do good things. It's just that the ward helps Mormons meet new people in a context where you're encouraged to do good things. It's a simple formula: The more connections you have, the more chances you have to help people when they need help. This mirrors one meaning of the word "religion," which comes from the Latin *re-ligare*, or "to bind together." Religions connect believers together, hopefully to do good.

Doing Good

In the first two chapters on goodness, we looked at different ways to know what is good. In this chapter we'll look at ways to put goodness into practice. After all, it's one thing to know what is good and another thing to act on it.

As Aristotle said, "We are not studying in order to know what virtue is, but to become good, for otherwise there would be no profit in it."

Many Mormons feel that their religion helps them become good in practical ways. I'm thinking of Richard Bushman, who was once asked by a Catholic theologian why he stayed in the Church despite knowing so much about its history. Bushman said, "I told him I remained a Mormon because when I followed my religion I became the kind of man I want to be. No philosophy, no evidence, nothing elaborate. Simply the personal reality that my religion helps me get better. That's what it comes down to in the crunch."

There's something to admire in this response. First, Bushman says that this is his "personal reality," indicating that he understands that this is not everyone's reality. Second, he earnestly values goodness. If more people were that sincere about wanting to become better, the world would be a more loving place.

Bushman's quote also highlights one reason why many active Mormons are sad when people leave:

They worry that those who leave will do less good in the world.

Is this worry valid? Do people who leave religious communities become the worse for it?

Social science shows that the answer isn't simple.

The Science of Goodness

To start, we must note that social scientists typically use the term *wellbeing* to describe the effects of goodness in a community. Wellbeing consists of positive societal and psychological qualities such as high life expectancy, good health, low crime rates, ample prosperity, solid educational attainment, and so on. So while they're not exactly synonyms, practical goodness brings about wellbeing.

So what have social scientists discovered?

On the one hand, a host of studies have found that religion does indeed bring goodness into people's lives. These studies show that people who are active participants in a religious community tend to be healthier, happier, and more charitable.[1] A range of studies also shows that churchgoers donate more time and money to both religious *and* secular causes.[2] As the psychologist Susan Pinker states, "Say what you like about religion, it has a way of bringing like-minded people together and binding them with songs, prayers, stories, and acts of kindness that make them feel good about themselves and the people around them."

And yet the evidence in favor of religious communities isn't clear-cut. For instance, one study of nearly 200,000 people in 11 European countries found that religious adherents have better wellbeing than the nonreligious—*but only in places where religious adherents are the dominant demographic.*[3] In places where secularism is dominant, the religious and the nonreligious fare equally well. In other words, where there is already a well-established secular community, the secular enjoy the same sense of wellbeing that the religious enjoy.

Other data show that wellbeing is actually *heightened* in secular societies. For instance, the sociologist Phil Zuckerman has mapped metrics of wellbeing to a society's level of secularism, and he has found that the more secular a society is, the higher that society tends to rank in terms of wellbeing.[4]

Specifically, Zuckerman shows that secular countries tend to have:

- Lower levels of corruption in business and government
- Lower rates of sexually transmitted disease
- Lower rates of aggravated assault
- Lower murder rates
- Lower teen pregnancy rates
- Lower environmental degradation
- Less pollution
- Higher quality of hospital care
- Higher quality of roads and highways
- Higher literacy rates
- Higher voter turnout
- Better sanitation
- Better access to clean drinking water

Zuckerman shows that the same results are true for states in the US as well. That is, less religious states (such as Maine, Vermont, Connecticut, New Hampshire, Rhode Island) tend to have better well-being than more religious states (such as Louisiana, Arkansas, Alabama, Mississippi, Georgia). In case after case, Zuckerman finds a correlation between secularism and heightened wellbeing.

Compromise and Doubt

What are we to make of all these conflicting studies?

First, we can see that there is goodness within religion and goodness outside of religion. That might sound obvious, but I still remember the first time this concept clicked for me. It was revolutionary. I mean, I always knew it was theoretically possible to have positive wellbeing without religion. But these studies suggested that *in real life* many secular people were doing just fine when it came to wellbeing. Learning this rattled my world. I finally internalized the fact that my religion didn't have a monopoly on morality. I realized that we are all in this together—clumsily trying our best to be good.

Second, we can see that goodness and community are closely correlated. Again, the study of 11 European countries showed that nonbelievers have greater wellbeing only in countries where secularism is dominant. Just like believers, nonbelievers fare better when they're part of a like-minded community.

This highlights a problem for those who doubt. It shows us that at some level, we all have to compromise no matter what community we belong to.

Without compromise, communities wouldn't exist. I say this because no individual perfectly agrees with every other individual in any group. We'd all be lonely, isolated, and friendless without compromise.

But that doesn't mean we should all go along blithely with everything our community does. In some cases, the right thing might be to oppose the moral lapses and errors of our community.

Indeed, many of my heroes throughout history are those who harbored serious doubts about the legitimacy of their mainstream community and even directly opposed it. They were clear-sighted enough to realize when the majority was not right.

Think of Socrates, who spent his life as a gadfly, peskily provoking the Athenian community to think harder, to question the assumptions behind what they thought of as common sense. His questioning spirit lived on in Plato, Aristotle, Epicurus, and Seneca, whose writings are foundational in Western philosophy and inspire people to live better lives today.

Or think of Jesus, whose contrarian words have led people all over the world to adopt an increased measure of compassion toward the poor and weary. Lines like "blessed are the meek" and "blessed are the poor in spirit" still stand in opposition to conventional wisdom today. In addition, the underlying message of so many teachings and parables from Jesus is that religion misapplied gets in the way of goodness. In this regard, Jesus epitomizes the contrarian hero.

The historical United States contains a lengthy list of contrarian heroes as well. Benjamin Franklin,

Thomas Paine, Frederick Douglass, Ralph Waldo Emerson, Henry David Thoreau, Abraham Lincoln, Mark Twain, Elizabeth Cady Stanton, Susan B. Anthony, Martin Luther King Jr., and Richard Feynman—all these people rejected the accepted wisdom of their time. And yet one could do far worse than to pattern one's life after these people. These are the people we talk about when we say that the heretics of one generation become the heroes of the next.

Importantly, these examples don't mean we should mindlessly oppose our communities. They just show that it isn't inherently immoral to do so.

I will revisit this point as it relates to Mormonism in the conclusion of this book. For now, I want to briefly return to the ideological theories of Jonathan Haidt. In *The Righteous Mind*, Haidt talks about the need for moral capital, which he defines as "the resources that sustain a moral community." He says that conservatives tend to be much better at preserving this kind of capital while liberals often overlook how important it is. We might say that conservatives tend to be better at compromising for the sake of their communities while liberals tend to be better at pointing out flaws in their communities.

Specifically, Haidt says, "Moral communities are fragile things, hard to build and easy to destroy. ... If you are trying to change an organization or a society and you do not consider the effects of your changes on moral capital you're asking for trouble. This, I believe, is the fundamental blind spot of the left. ... It is the reason I believe that liberalism—which has done so much to bring about freedom and equal opportunity—is not sufficient as a governing philosophy. It tends to overreach, change too many things too quickly, and reduce the stock of moral capital inadvertently. Conversely, while conservatives do a better job of preserving moral capital, they often fail to notice certain classes of victims, fail to limit the predations of certain powerful interests, and fail to see the need to change or update institutions as times change."

In other words, compromise and doubt aren't absolute goods. Compromise is the necessary process of sustaining communities. Doubt is the necessary process of refining the flaws in communities. By working in conjunction, both of these processes improve the wellbeing of humanity. Both are essential. Both have tradeoffs.

This concept matters because when we admit that there are tradeoffs to our position, we can admit that the people who disagree with us aren't hopelessly misguided. In sum, whether we lean toward compromise or lean toward doubt, this is a concept that can help us save our relationships.

Beauty, Part 3

THE TROUBLE WITH BEAUTY

"The truth is not always beautiful, nor beautiful words the truth."
—LAO TZU

A Strange, Peaceful Night

The summer before I left on my mission, I worked at a small video rental store that had almost zero customers. As a result, I spent a lot of time sitting at the counter, reading.

One day I decided that I would read the Book of Mormon. All day. I wanted to feel something that would solidify the truth of the book before I was sent to testify about it as a missionary. So I read it for eight hours straight, all afternoon and all evening.

As night descended and I read alone in the room, I felt a quiet sense of peace.

Then something strange happened. An enormous swarm of gnats flew in through a door I had propped open. They bounced spasmodically against the ceiling light, rapidly striking it over and over. Not knowing quite what to do but not wanting my desk to be caked with the carcasses of gnats the next day, I pulled the vacuum out of the closet and sucked them all up with the hose.

A few hours later, when I went to leave, I couldn't find the key to the outside door.

I searched for about a half an hour, and then I decided to call my mom, who knew what to do in these situations far better than I did. She said she would drive down to help.

In the meantime, I thought I must have somehow vacuumed the key up when I suctioned the gnats. So I decided to pull out the vacuum and open the vacuum bag.

The moment I opened the bag, the entire swarm of gnats flew out and back up to the ceiling. I dug my hands through the thick dust and dirt in the bag and didn't find the key anywhere.

I zipped the bag up. Then I had to once again vacuum up all the gnats.

My mom arrived soon after and helped me search for another ten minutes, but we still couldn't find the key. So I locked the bolt from the inside, climbed out a window, and then slid the window as shut as I could get it.

Here's the point of this story. Normally I would have felt angry and upset during the whole event with the gnats and the lost key. I would have been flustered by how annoying the situation was. But this time I didn't feel that way. I just observed it unfolding. I did my best to solve the problem, but I didn't let it get to me. I even told my mom that I loved her as we left, which is something, unfortunately, that I hardly ever did.

As strange as it might sound, this is the experience I used as a reference point when I bore testimony about the Book of Mormon while I was on my mission.

I knew that I had felt profound peace when I read the Book of Mormon that day, and that was sufficient for me to tell other people I knew the book was true.

While this story with the gnats is unique to me, there's something universal about this experience. For centuries, people have interpreted feelings of awe and peace as proof that their beliefs are true.

The Division between Truth and Beauty

In the last chapter about beauty we looked at how people all over the world have powerful spiritual experiences that help them live more fully.

In this chapter we look at more examples of people having spiritual experiences, but in these instances we see how people use these experiences to justify the truthfulness of a tradition they'd like to belong to.

William James calls this experience "conversion," and he notes that "the persons who have passed through conversion, having once taken a stand for the religious life, tend to feel themselves identified with it." That is, spiritual experiences are often directly interwoven with a person's religious identity.

To illustrate how this process works, let's first look at how Americans in the early 1800s talked about spiritual experiences as being foundational to their chosen faiths.

One woman attended a camp meeting and had a profoundly moving moment where she saw "beauty in every material object." This happened around the same time that Joseph Smith was attending camp meetings as a young man in New York. It gives us a sense of the religious fervor of his time, making this woman's story even more relevant to Mormons. She said, "I was taken to a camp-meeting, mother and religious friends seeking and praying for my conversion. My emotional nature was stirred to its depths; confessions of depravity and pleading with God for salvation from sin made me oblivious of all surroundings. ... It was like entering another world, a new state of existence. Natural objects were glorified, my spiritual vision was so clarified that I saw beauty in every material object in the universe, the woods were vocal with heavenly music; my soul exulted in the love of God, and I wanted everybody to share in my joy."[1]

Another man from the same era describes his experience as seeing a light "like the brightness of the sun."

He said, "All at once the glory of God shone upon and round about me in a manner almost marvelous. ... A light perfectly ineffable shone in my soul, that almost prostrated me on the ground. ... This light seemed like the brightness of the sun in every direction. It was too intense for the eyes. ... I think I knew something then, by actual experience, of that light that prostrated Paul on the way to Damascus. It was surely a light such as I could not have endured long."[2]

Since most of these early American accounts come from believing Christians, the stories often center on Jesus. The story of Stephen Bradley, for instance, happens to reflect some of the same sentiments from Joseph Smith. Like Smith, Bradley was 14 years old in 1820 when he said he saw Jesus. Bradley said, "I thought I saw the Saviour, by faith, in human shape, for about one second in the room, with arms extended, appearing to say to me, Come. The next day I rejoiced with trembling; soon after, my happiness was so great that I said that I wanted to die; this world had no place in my affections, as I knew of, and every day appeared as solemn to me as the Sabbath. I had an ardent desire that all mankind might feel as I did; I wanted to have them all love God supremely. Previous to this time I was very selfish and self-righteous; but now I desired the welfare of all mankind."[3]

Again, we see that people improve their desires as a result of these religious experiences, but we also see that all of these experiences were used to validate truth claims—specifically the truth of Christianity.

Modern Examples

Alvin Plantinga, a religious philosopher who taught at the University of Notre Dame, spent two semesters at Harvard University as an undergraduate. There he came face to face with a host of students and professors who held beliefs that differed from his own. After hearing the reasons for their beliefs, he began to doubt whether his own beliefs "could really be true."

These doubts pressed hard on Plantinga's mind for several weeks until he had an experience that brought resolution and renewed his faith in God. He said, "One gloomy evening (in January, perhaps) I was returning from dinner, walking past Widener Library to my fifth-floor room in Thayer Middle ... It was dark, windy, raining, nasty. But suddenly it was as if the heavens opened; I heard, so it seemed, music of overwhelming power and grandeur and sweetness; there was light of unimaginable splendor and *beauty*; it seemed I could see into heaven itself; and I suddenly saw or perhaps felt with great clarity and persuasion and conviction that the Lord was really there."[4]

In short, Plantinga was walking on Harvard campus and had a sudden religious experience that solidified his belief that Christianity was in fact true. Shortly after that, he left Harvard and studied at Calvin College, where he started his career as a Christian philosopher.

Here's another story, this one from a scientist named Francis Collins, who led the human genome project. For years Collins had felt that being an atheist left him unfulfilled, and so he spent considerable time reading and reflecting on C. S. Lewis's book *Mere Christianity*, wanting to believe in a god of comfort. Somewhere in the middle of his wrestling, he went on a hike and experienced the sublime. He said, "On a beautiful fall day, as I was hiking in the Cascade Mountains during my first trip west of the Mississippi, the majesty and *beauty* of God's creation overwhelmed my resistance. As I rounded a corner and saw a beautiful and unexpected frozen waterfall, hundreds of feet high, I knew the search was over."[5] The waterfall had three frozen parts to it, which Collins interpreted as proof of a Trinitarian god (Father, Son, and Holy Ghost). Based on that interpretation, he converted to evangelical Christianity, a decision he maintained for the rest of his life.

Stories like these certainly aren't limited to Christianity. One documentarian collected a range of testimonies from around the world, many of which I cite in this chapter.[6] For instance, a Muslim man said, "I was making supplication: Allah help me, guide me, guide me to the truth. If you guide me to the truth, I'll never leave it. And I knew in my heart—Allah was telling me in my heart—that Islam is true. And I knew right then that it was the correct religion."

Similarly, a Muslim woman said, "I started praying to find the truth. It doesn't take a long time to find out that Islam is the truth, and that there can't be any other religion in the world." And another, speaking of the Qur'an, said, "I could not stop reading it. It was, like, feeding me." Then she said, in tears, "And that's when I knew I wanted to become Muslim."

Another Muslim woman told her story this way: "I said, God, you are the one who listens, who always listens. Please, who do I have to follow to come to you directly—Christianity, or the Muslim faith? ... I'm one-hundred percent sure that God has answered my question. What is the right way, the only right way to come to God? Islam."[7]

A convert to Judaism said that she experienced a "very strong overwhelming feeling" when she started to study about the religion. She wanted to convert when she went to a synagogue for the first time and, in her words, "immediately felt comfortable even though I did not know anyone."[8] And another convert to Judaism said that his decision felt "like the simple and irrational process of falling in love."[9] Another said, "I started to do a lot of reading [about Judaism] and very quickly the pieces started to fall together. I felt like I had found my way home."[10]

One more example: AJ Miller, a contemporary religious leader, says that he is Jesus Christ in the flesh and that he has returned to Earth. He tells his followers not to trust his word directly, but to instead ask God whether or not what he says is true. He says that "there is a general process that God designed that allows us to discover what is truth and what is not. The process would be: Ask this God to receive love, and then feel about that particular thing. And if that particular thing turns off the flow, I know it's not true. And if that particular thing stays flowing, then I know it's true."

One of Miller's followers testified on camera about his experience trying out this process and said that he had gained a testimony that Miller was indeed who he said he was. This follower said, "Whenever I think about him now, I just cry. I'm starting to have this whole emotional realization of who he is. It's overwhelming."[11]

In this same vein, a young fundamentalist Mormon bore her testimony at a church meeting, saying,

"I've been searching for a witness of this work and of this Church, and just tonight I got my witness. It's burning within my soul, how important this work is, how *true* it is. I know it is. And it's hard to believe that just a year ago I was in high school, and now I'm in a plural marriage and... struggling. But I know, without a shadow of a doubt, that this is the Lord's work, that I have finally found it. I say this in the name of Jesus Christ, Amen."[12] This young lady believes in the truth of the FLDS religion because of a "burning" within the soul, despite the fact that she openly admits the religion is making her miserable.

The process described over and over here echoes the process described in Moroni's promise in the Book of Mormon. "I would exhort you that ye would ask God, the Eternal Father, in the name of Christ, if these things are not true; and if ye shall ask with a sincere heart, with real intent, having faith in Christ, he will manifest the truth of it unto you." As we've seen, this is the process that religious people all over the world use to figure out whether their beliefs are true.

The Trouble of Pursuing Beauty without Truth
Unfortunately, sometimes people who conflate beauty with truth end up facing very disturbing consequences.

Here are three stories to illustrate the point.

1.
A Jehovah's Witness couple had a baby that needed a blood transfusion, and they struggled to know what

to do. The father said, "If we freely gave our daughter a blood transfusion, we'd be excommunicated."

They said the doctor told them that they had to choose to either give their child a blood transfusion or watch their child die. The father said, "I remember going over to the bed where she had these cords and wires keeping her alive, and holding this limp child that was our only daughter. I went over to the window and looked out at the clouds in the sky and said, 'Oh God, Jehovah,' and I started to weep."

Then the mother said, "We just had a real distinct impression that we were supposed to obey God's law and go by what we had always been taught, and that we were to let our daughter die."

2.

Marshall Applewhite started a religious following in the 1970s called Heaven's Gate—a movement that eventually ended in the suicide of 39 members in 1997. Here is the method he used to invite his followers to know whether what he said were true. "At least ponder this," he said. "That you go into the privacy of your closet. Don't ask your neighbors, your friends. You go see if you can connect with the purest, highest source that you might consider God. And say, 'What about this? Is this for real?'"

One of Applewhite's followers acted on his advice to pay attention to God's voice, which convinced her that Applewhite's followers were of God. She said, "When I first met them I knew that what they had to say was true. It wasn't something they said. It was something I knew inside me."

Another follower claimed that "it was an instant recognition for me, and there was never a doubt in my mind. I just wish people out there could understand how much we feel and know this is real. ... This is not a fantasy ... I didn't have to believe. I *knew*."[13]

3.

Jim Jones, founder of the Peoples Temple, also convinced people to rely on their feelings instead of their intellects. His followers had tremendous emotional experiences. One follower said, "the Peoples Temple services, they had life, they had soul, they had power. We were alive in those services."[14]

Another follower said, "I have never been so totally happy or fulfilled in my life. I can't begin to describe it. You could sit here and talk all day long and no words could describe the peace, the *beauty*, the sense of accomplishment and responsibility and camaraderie that's here. It's overwhelming, it really is. You can't describe it."

These people were experiencing beauty, but they left reason at the door—a mistake that created hell on earth.

They couldn't see that the healings in Peoples Temple were staged. They couldn't see that Jim Jones planted employees in the audience who pretended to be healed. They couldn't admit that behind all the talk of a post-racial world and having all things in common (Jones was very progressive on both fronts), Jones was making a habit of abusive sexual practices. His followers couldn't bring themselves to concede that their leader would really poison them and their children to death.

It all spiraled downhill in Jonestown on November 18, 1978, after Jim Jones had sent an armed group to slaughter a visiting Congressman and a group of reporters. That was when Jones administered cyanide-laced Kool-Aid to his followers, first to the children.

One follower who survived described the scene in the most nightmarish terms imaginable: "As I walked up to the back of the pavilion, I saw a woman name Rosie on the ground crying. ... There were maybe eight or nine other people who were dying, or in the process of dying. Inside, I just wanted things to stop. Please, just let me catch my breath; let me figure out what's happening here. ... My wife died in my arms and my dead baby son was in her arms. And I held her and said, "I love you, I love you," because it's all I could say."

There's a line in that description—"Just let me catch my breath; let me figure out what's happening here"—that perfectly encapsulates what was going on between Jim Jones and his followers. Jones didn't give his followers room to think. He wanted no room for intellectual curiosity because he knew that even slight questioning would cut his power completely. He wanted all the trappings of beauty without any truth.

We Need More Beauty and Less Interpretation

What lessons can we take from these stories?

First, we can see that people all over the world

interpret feelings of profound beauty as proof that their beliefs are true. Moroni's promise is not unique to Mormonism.

Second, it's clear that when we interpret beautiful experiences, we have a strong tendency to either privilege the beliefs we were raised with or the beliefs we've been investigating. For instance, it's unlikely that someone who has never heard of Islam will interpret a beautiful experience as proof that Islam is true, but it *is* likely that someone who has been raised as a devote Muslim will. Our interpretation of beauty always hinges on our prior experience and knowledge.

Third, it's clear that not all interpretations of beautiful experiences are valid. If a Muslim and a Christian both say that their beautiful experience is proof that their religion is the only true religion, they can't both be right.

Fourth, interpreting beauty as truth can sometimes lead to horrifying results. This is the case especially in religious circles that double down on rhetoric about the end of the world.

Fifth, and most simply, human beings don't do a great job of attaching meaning to beautiful experiences.

Taken together, all these lessons point to the conclusion that we need more beauty and less interpretation. Instead of using beautiful experiences as proof that our beliefs are true, it would be better to use them to develop our sense of gratitude and love. Gratitude and love are more than sufficient.

It's also critical to keep in mind that if we discover that some of our beliefs aren't true, it doesn't diminish the reality of our beautiful experiences in the least. The experiences were real. We just need to keep in mind that our interpretation of the beautiful experiences were likely colored by our knowledge and desires. We must realize, as Lao Tzu once said, that "the truth is not always beautiful, nor beautiful words the truth."

Above all, we must continue to seek for beauty. In a world where we're often tucked away in beige cubicles all day, where city planning is thoughtless and ugly, where vapid television programs blare on for hours, we need more beauty. We must seek for art, film, architecture, and music that can lift our emotional centers. We must nurture stillness.

Truth, Part 3

MORE THAN LITERAL MEANING

"Metaphors help eliminate what separates you and me."
—HARUKI MURAKAMI

The Old Testament

About a decade ago, I decided to read the Old Testament the whole way through in a summer.

When I told a friend (a well-read and active Mormon) about my goal, her response surprised me. She said, "Yeah, maybe I should read it the whole way through too." But then she quickly changed her mind, saying, "Actually, to be honest, I don't think I ever will. There are too many other books on my list."

There are too many other books on my list.

At the time, I thought, "Of *course* you should read it the whole way through. It's one of the few books on Earth directly inspired by God. There are few books more important to read before you die."

And then I read it the whole way through and realized she may have had a point.

If you've studied the Old Testament in detail, you know it's a mixed bag. It contains some beautiful moments, such as the story of David weeping over the death of Absalom or the story of Ruth's commitment to Naomi. But it also contains an abundance of horrors, many which are directly attributed to God.

As Mormon writer Michael Ash says, "The scriptures relate the stories of God's people, but not everything these people did was instructed by God—even though they may have thought it was at the time."

In the story of Judges 19–21, for instance, the Israelites say that God tells them to relentlessly pursue a civil war to the point that they kill every woman, child, and animal in all of Benjamin. They almost succeed in killing every man in Benjamin too, but 600 soldiers escape. Then, when the Israelites realize that they've almost completely killed off an entire tribe, they steal all the virgins from the city of Jabesh (and slaughter everyone else there) so the Benjamites can keep reproducing.

Equally horrific, the narrator in Numbers chapter 16 claims that God opened up the earth to swallow a family who disagreed with Moses. Then God burns alive 250 rebellious priests, and when the people complain that burning humans alive is a cruel thing to do, God kills 14,700 of them with the plague.

There are many more examples. In Deuteronomy, the Lord condones acts of genocide, including child slaughter against foreigners, and he gets so angry at the Israelites that he refuses to help them even when they plead for it (and even though he has the power to help them). Altogether, the death count attributed to God in the Old Testament is nearly three million people.[1]

After reading the Old Testament, I was struck by how much the text feels as though it were written long ago by tribal men who couldn't make sense of a brutal world—a world with drought, earthquakes, and floods—and who therefore attributed this brutality to an angry God.

Importantly, this doesn't mean that the entire Old Testament isn't true (a statement that is too sweeping for a book containing dozens of different authors, ancient wisdom, glimpses of history, lengthy poetry, and folklore). However, it does mean that we have to read the Old Testament in the context of the time it was written and recognize that the text consists of a mix of bloody history and brutal folklore, a mix of truth and metaphor. We have to take a measured approach instead of viewing the text as either the infallible word of God or as a work of complete falsehood. We have to remember that the book was written by people who had their own points of view and their own lessons to teach.

But what about the New Testament? Is it also colored by human views?

The New Testament

In this chapter, I look at what biblical scholars have discovered about the New Testament and what it means for us today. As with the chapter on Mormonism, I feel nervous about the content. It has the potential to open rifts, which is the opposite of what I'm hoping for.

However, again, we can't agree to unite around ignorance. If it turns out that biblical scholars have discovered compelling reasons that the history of the New Testament is more complex than we may have thought, then we should know about those reasons. That's the only way for us to save our relationships and simultaneously be honest in our pursuit of the truth. We must lean into discomfort.

Importantly, nothing in this chapter leads to the conclusion that people should leave Mormonism. By contrast, I learned most of this content through a Mormon Sunday School teacher who recommended a series of books to me about New Testament history and who taught this content openly in his Sunday School class. His class brought some of my most spiritually profound moments that year. For me, the historical view of the New Testament has been a source of great happiness as I've studied it in detail. I have found the core of New Testament teachings, and they are wonderful.

Another thing worth noting is that this information has been known for many decades, even though it hasn't yet made its way into most Mormon Sunday School lessons. For instance, Martin Luther King Jr. learned about these topics when he got his PhD in theology, and at first these topics troubled him. He said, "My college training, especially the first two years, brought many doubts into my mind.

It was then that the shackles of fundamentalism were removed from my body. More and more I could see a gap between what I had learned in Sunday school and what I was learning in college. ... This conflict continued until I studied a course in Bible in which I came to see that behind the legends and myths of the Book were many profound truths which one could not escape."[2]

These profound truths helped King fight for greater justice and love.

In a similar vein, I hope the knowledge in this chapter is more inspiring than devastating, more motivating than aggravating. I hope it moves believers and nonbelievers to unite around the pursuit of truth.

***

Let's start by looking at how the New Testament came to be. Then we can delve into specific stories that are more likely metaphor than fact.

This idea isn't as controversial within Mormonism as it might sound since Mormons "believe the Bible to be the word of God as far as it is translated correctly"—a statement that indicates Mormons already believe that sections of the Bible aren't completely accurate.

But which sections aren't accurate? Is there even one verse in the King James Version (KJV) of the Bible that we can say for sure doesn't belong?

Fortunately, we can answer those questions today.

To date, historians have collected more than twenty thousand complete or fragmented ancient biblical manuscripts written in a multiplicity of languages. By studying a range of characteristics (including the materials the manuscripts were written on and the way the text was written), scholars have pinned down which centuries these manuscripts were written in.

Here's what they've found:

- Most existing manuscripts were written after 900 AD
- Manuscripts written from 200–800 AD are *incredibly* rare
- No manuscripts exist from 30–125 AD that we know of

What this means is that we don't have any of the original New Testament manuscripts. We also don't have the copies of the originals. In fact, as biblical scholar Bart Ehrman notes, "We don't even have copies of the copies of the copies of the originals." All we have are copies that, in most cases, were transcribed hundreds of years after the originals were written. And scholars have located 200,000 to 400,000 differences among all the various copies.[3]

Because of all these differences, we don't know for sure which single manuscript is the most accurate. However, we do know one thing for sure: It isn't the KJV. Although the language in the KJV is beautiful, it's based on subpar twelfth century manuscripts and therefore contains a range of transcription errors and verses that were added by early scribes.

For instance, 1 John 5:7 didn't exist in the earliest manuscripts. Mormons might be glad to know that this verse was added later since it seems to support the concept of the Trinity:

For there are three that bear record in heaven, the Father, the Word, and the Holy Ghost: and these three are one.

Here's another example, from the story of Jesus healing people at the pool of Bethesda, found in John 5:3–4:

In these lay a great multitude of impotent folk, of blind, halt, withered, *waiting for the moving of the water. For an angel went down at a certain season into the pool, and troubled the water: whosoever then first after the troubling of the water stepped in was made whole of whatsoever disease he had.*

Everything in italics—all the stuff about the angel seasonally troubling the waters —surfaced only in later manuscripts. Someone thought it should be added, and other copyists agreed or didn't know better. Then it made its way through the medieval manuscripts into the KJV.

There are so many more examples that we could spend the rest of the chapter detailing them. Let's look at just one more here.

The KJV includes Mark 16:9–20 even though the earliest and most reliable manuscripts don't have those verses. They were added later. Originally, the book of Mark ended at 16:8. In that version, the final verses tell of Mary Magdalene, Mary the mother of James, and Salome visiting the tomb and seeing an angel who tells them that Jesus has risen from the grave.

> 6. And he said unto them, "Be not afraid. Ye seek Jesus of Nazareth, who was crucified. He is risen! He is not here. Behold the place where they laid Him.
> 7. But go your way. Tell His disciples and Peter that He goeth before you into Galilee. There shall ye see Him, as He said unto you."
> 8. And they went out quickly and fled from the sepulcher, for they trembled and were amazed; neither said they any thing to any man, for they were afraid.

That's hardly a satisfying ending, is it? The three women run away and don't tell anyone what the angel said. It's certainly not solid proof that Jesus was resurrected, which was the main contention in early Christianity. So someone came in later and added Mark 16:9–20, which says that other people saw the risen Jesus and that Jesus told his followers to do missionary work and essentially start a church. That ending was much more satisfying to believers, and it ended up being the one that made it into the mainstream manuscripts going forward.

Here's the point: Certain verses were added to later manuscripts. Contemporary biblical scholars agree on this front so universally that when you look at modern translations of the Bible (including those used widely by evangelical Christians), the added verses have footnotes openly acknowledging that the verses were late additions.

"But that's just what the scholars say," someone might assert. "Why should we trust them?"

We have to recognize that in all cases we're trusting scholars. The people who translated the KJV were scholars; the people who analyze biblical passages today are scholars. The difference is that contemporary scholars have far greater access to manuscripts and metadata than scholars during the reign of King James did.

In other words, during the 400 years since the KJV was completed, we've uncovered more manuscripts and learned more about language and history. Our understanding is still flawed, but it's better than it was back then. Why not trust today's scholarship more? We don't trust medical science from the 1600s. We should be similarly wary of biblical scholarship from that era.

Compiling the Gospels

To really understand how the New Testament came to be, we must travel back much further than the 1600s. We must understand how the Gospels themselves were compiled.

First, we must note that we have no record of anything written by Jesus or anything written about him while he was alive. The earliest writings we have about Jesus were written roughly 20 years after his death by someone who never met him: Paul of Tarsus.

Second, the Gospels were written to prove that Jesus was the Messiah (i.e., the person who would liberate the Jews). During this era, many people—including Simon of Perea, Athronges, and Judas of Galilee—claimed to be the Messiah and were also swiftly executed by the Romans. The Gospels were therefore written to establish that the other messiahs weren't legitimate and that Jesus was the one and only true Messiah.

Third, the Gospels were based on the oral traditions of Jesus's earliest followers. These early followers were almost certainly illiterate since they were part of the peasant class.

It wasn't until Christianity gained a number of educated converts that the traditions were written down. The first Gospel chronologically is named after Mark and was written roughly thirty years after Jesus's death, while the last Gospel, named after John, was written roughly 70 years after Jesus's death.

The chronology looks like this:

- Mark: 60–70 AD
- Matthew: 70–80 AD
- Luke: 70–80 AD
- John: 90–100 AD

Several other Gospels were also written around the same era, including the Gospel of Mary and the Gospel of Judas, but only four—the four we have today—were deemed legitimate by an early Catholic pope.

Contradictions in the Gospels

During the approximately 40 years between Mark and John, many things changed about the story of Jesus—some of which are directly contradictory. A few of the contradictions are worth noting here because they illustrate the complexity of finding the truth about the New Testament. In certain cases we have to look at what the original manuscripts said because later manuscripts were altered to bring uniformity to the narratives.

The general trend is that the narratives get more and more grand as time goes on. Mark's Gospel is pretty straightforward and brief. Matthew and Luke used Mark for much of their source material (along with other sources that are now lost) and made the story a little grander and more miraculous. Most miraculous of all is the Gospel of John.

In addition, the Gospels become more and more anti-Semitic as time goes on, which fits with the trend that Christians were increasingly trying to separate themselves from the Jews so they could gain favor with the Romans. For instance, John refers to "the Jews" 71 times (compared to 16 times by Matthew, Mark, and Luke combined), and the references are frequently hostile and negative.[4] Many of these verses have been used by Christians to mistreat the Jews over the centuries.

I remember how surprised I was the first time I learned about these differences among the Gospels.

Here I had read the Gospels dozens of times in my life, and yet I had never picked up on the distinctions among the accounts. What I realized is that the differences are transparent only when you read the same story in each Gospel side by side instead of reading the Gospels straight through—reading horizontally rather than vertically, as some scholars say. This horizontal reading reveals that the Gospels are consistently dissimilar and frequently contradictory.

Below are examples from the hundreds of possible choices. Note that I have italicized certain passages to emphasize the differences.

The Voice at Jesus's Baptism
- Mark: "Thou art my beloved son, in whom I am well pleased."
- Matthew: "This is my beloved son, in whom I am well pleased."
- Luke (in the oldest manuscripts): "Thou art my son, *today I have begotten thee.*" In this version, Jesus is begotten of God when he is baptized.
- John: Not mentioned.

After Jesus's Baptism
- Mark: Jesus meets with John the Baptist and then "immediately" goes to the wilderness for 40 days.
- John: Jesus meets with John the Baptist, and then he gathers his disciples "the next day" rather than going into the wilderness.

Jesus and Jarius's Daughter

- Mark: Jarius asks Jesus for help, saying, "My little daughter *lieth at the point of death*. I pray thee, come and lay thy hands on her, that she may be healed." In other words, Jesus heals a sick girl.

- Matthew: Jarius asks Jesus for help, saying, "My daughter is *even now dead*: but come and lay thy hand upon her, and she shall live." In this version, Jesus raises a girl from the dead—a much grander miracle.

Pontius Pilate

- Mark: Pilate doesn't say that Jesus is innocent.

- John: Pilate tells the Jews three times that Jesus is innocent, an action that by implication removes the blame from the Romans and places it on the Jews. This is in line with the idea that as Christianity grew, it distanced itself from Judaism to make the religion more appealing to the Romans.

Jesus's Post-Resurrection Appearances

- Mark (oldest manuscripts): Jesus appears to no one.

- Matthew: Jesus appears to Mary Magdalene and the other Mary and then to the eleven disciples.

- Luke/Acts: Jesus appears to disciples (no

women), and for forty days he appears to the Apostles.

- John: Jesus appears to Mary Magdalene and then his disciples. He later reappears to his disciples.

Based on the sheer number of added verses and contradictions (there are many more that I didn't cover here), we know that the Gospels as we currently have them are flawed in very specific and fundamental ways.

Some people don't want to accept this fact because it means the truth is far more complicated than they once supposed. It requires figuring out which verses are legitimate. It's potentially a lot of work. Plus, it opens up a rabbit hole. If you accept that even one verse isn't legitimate, then you accept the possibility that other verses aren't legitimate either. Where does it end?

More Than Literal Meaning

Perhaps the best way forward is to keep in mind that the Gospels weren't meant to be mere historical documents. Instead, each Gospel writer had a goal in mind and therefore intentionally mixed real scenarios with metaphor, similar to how Jesus crafted his parables. John Dominic Crossan, a notable biblical scholar, describes the Gospels by saying, "parables by Jesus became parables about Jesus."[5]

Biblical scholar Marcus Borg adds that these parables have a "more than literal meaning" that can change our lives in powerful ways, completely independent of factual validity—similar to how poetry can change lives.[6]

To illustrate how this works with poetry, take the first stanza of Emily Dickinson's poem "Because I could not stop for Death":

> Because I could not stop for Death—
> He kindly stopped for me—
> The Carriage held but just Ourselves—
> And Immortality.

By personifying death and immortality and putting them both in a carriage, Dickinson makes these concepts less terrifying—perhaps helping us calm the existential anxiety they bring. It's true that death is not really a stagecoach driver and immortality can't fit in a carriage. But that doesn't mean the poem itself is "false." The poem instead has a more than literal meaning. It functions in the realm of metaphor instead of the realm of fact.

The writers of the Gospels deliberately wrote in this same way. They were primarily focused on what they saw as beauty, not objective historical truth. They colored the text with their personal view in the process. (For more on this topic, I recommend reading the work of John Dominic Crossan and Marcus Borg—both of whom write with exceptional empathy.)

The Beauty of the Truth

Why does any of this matter? For me, learning about the nuances of the New Testament has freed me up to the possibility that I don't have to blindly accept everything in the Gospels as, well, the gospel truth.

I might suggest that with this knowledge comes the freedom to not internalize the New Testament's cruelest and most divisive sentiments. I don't have to fixate on the view that the world is about to end and that God will literally set wicked people on fire. I don't have to divide the world into sheep and goats, where I am a sheep and the people who don't share my beliefs are goats. I don't have to harbor anxiety that I might never be forgiven in this world nor in the world to come for denying the Holy Ghost, a needlessly vague sin that has likely caused millions of people throughout history to live with the fear they've committed it.

And then there are the 2,000 pigs Jesus is said to have sent to their deaths, the fig tree he kills, and the passages where he is portrayed as mean-spirited and cruel to his family. Every time I have gone on a self-righteous tirade, thinking I'm justified because I'm reprimanding evildoers just as Jesus did, I have felt guilt and regret.

By contrast, I have never regretted following the most generous impulses of the New Testament, many of which are found in the Sermon on the Mount:

"Love your enemies, bless them that curse you, do good to them that hate you, and pray for them which despitefully use you, and persecute you."

"For if ye love them which love you, what reward have ye? ... And if ye salute your brethren only, what do ye more than others?"

"Judge not, that you be not judged."

"Why beholdest thou the mote that is in thy brother's eye, but considerest not the beam that is in thine own eye?"

"Where your treasure is, there will your heart be also."

"Whatsoever ye would that men should do to you, do ye even so to them."

There are so many more.

In conclusion, it's clear that the Bible contains verses that are products of their time as well as many verses that are far ahead of their time—verses we still haven't internalized over 2,000 years later. The Bible also contains many verses that have more than literal meaning and are powerful on the level of beauty.

The Bible can divide us, or it can bring us together and fill us with love for one another. I hope we choose the latter. This is the message I take from biblical scholarship.

A Conclusion in Three Parts

THE FOUNDATION AND FUTURE OF TRUTH, BEAUTY, AND GOODNESS

> *"Have patience with everything that remains unsolved in your heart. Try to love the questions themselves."*
> —RAINER RILKE

> *"The secret of living well is not in having all the answers but in pursuing unanswerable questions in good company."*
> —RACHEL REMEN

> *"From the standpoint of daily life, there is one thing we do know: that we are here for the sake of each other."*
> —ALBERT EINSTEIN

Part I: Death Inspires Reverence

The business tycoon Ted Leonsis became a millionaire in his early twenties, and everything seemed just about perfect. He bought cars. He bought houses. He spent his time trying to impress girls.

Then, unexpectedly, he faced his own death.

He boarded a plane that malfunctioned midflight. Nothing seemed right. The pilot got on the intercom and told the passengers that they would need to prepare for a crash landing.

Many passengers started crying, and Leonsis felt desperate. He asked himself, "What's my strength? What am I going to do?" He decided that he had no choice but to pray. He directed his thoughts to what he named his "higher calling" and said, "If you let me live through this, I'll leave more than I take, and I will try to make this next part of my life more meaningful to the world and not just to me."

Thankfully, the pilot regained control and landed the plane safely. Still, the experience shook Leonsis deeply. The following weekend, he sat down and reflected on the purpose of his life. He asked himself, "If I had to write my obituary, how would I keep score?" Based on that question, he made a list of 101 things he wanted to do before he died, including tasks such as "take care of my mother and father" and "give away $100 million in my lifetime." The list became his guidepost for the following decades.

He started to live for more than himself.

Leonsis's story mirrors the story of Ebenezer Scrooge in *A Christmas Carol*. Scrooge accumulated piles of wealth and lived only for himself. Then, one Christmas, he faced a series of ghosts, culminating in the Ghost of Christmas Yet To Come. This ghost showed Scrooge his own impending funeral. When Scrooge saw that no one cared that he had died, he woke up and reformed his habits, living a life of generosity.

Remembering that we'll all die wakes us up to what really matters.

It's a lesson that goes back thousands of years. As the Roman emperor Marcus Aurelius noted, "Do not act as if you were going to live ten thousand years. Death hangs over you. While you live, while it is in your power, be good." The poet Horace said, "Believe that each day that dawns may be your last." And the philosopher Seneca said, "Begin at once to live, and count each separate day as a separate life."

Leo Tolstoy put it bluntly when he stated, "If a person knows that he will die in a half hour, he certainly will not bother doing trivial, stupid, or, especially, bad things during this half hour. Perhaps you have half a century before you die—what makes this any different from a half hour?"

It might seem backwards, but reflecting on the vulnerable nature of our humanity puts us in a state of mind to live a quality life. Steve Jobs once said, "Remembering that I'll be dead soon is the most important tool I've ever encountered to help me make the big choices in life. Almost everything—all external expectations, all pride, all fear of embarrassment or failure—these things just fall away in the face of death, leaving only what is truly important."

In this same vein, the *New York Times* columnist David Brooks says that focusing on death causes us to shift from a life centered in "résumé virtues" to a life centered in "eulogy virtues."

Résumé virtues, as you might guess, are virtues that look good on a résumé: *Graduated top of the class, managed a team of 20 people, learned a foreign language*, for example. These virtues are important when it comes to earning an income, but people don't care much about them when you die.

By contrast, eulogy virtues are about generosity. What did you contribute to the world? How did you treat other people? Where did you bring joy?

Life before Death
"Don't be afraid of death so much as an inadequate life." —Bertolt Brecht

The French writer Michel Montaigne was terrified of death in his twenties and early thirties. He read ancient philosophers who wrote about death, and he witnessed the deaths of his father and his best friend. As a result, he was weighed down by the realization that anyone could die at any moment.

Eventually he faced death himself. He was riding his horse down a path when another rider's horse went wild and slammed into him, sending him crashing to the ground. As Montaigne dropped in and out of consciousness, blood rivered down his shirt and filled him with horror. He later wrote, "It seemed to me that my life was hanging only by the tip of my lips."

Over the next several months, Montaigne healed and shook his anxiety about dying. He realized that there was no point in worrying about death. It would come when it would. There was nothing he could do about it. "If you don't know how to die, don't worry," he wrote. "Nature will tell you what to do on the spot, fully and adequately. She will do this job perfectly for you; don't bother your head about it."

"Don't bother your head about it" became something of a motto for Montaigne. He decided that his brush with death would be a catalyst for truly living. He let go of his anxiety and changed the course of his life. No longer did he merely fulfill his household duties as he had done for decades. Instead he did what he felt he was meant to do with his life: he began writing.

Just like that, Michel Montaigne chose a life that was in tune with his true self, and the world became a far better place as a result. His brilliant essays remain in print today and still help people live better lives.

The lesson from Montaigne is that if reflecting on death makes us morose, we're doing it wrong. Death shouldn't turn us into wheezing goths, pensive and anxiety-riddled. Rather, it should inspire us to practice humility and reverence.

Death Inspires Reverence

In Mormonism, the word "reverent" is used as a synonym for "quiet." When you hear this word, you might visualize a young child folding his arms at the front of a Primary room. Maybe you think of the Primary song "Reverently, Quietly."

While being quiet is a good thing in a busy and loud world, the word "reverent" has a bigger meaning. It comes from the Latin word *reverentia*, which means "to stand in awe of something."

As the philosopher Paul Woodruff says, "Reverence begins in a deep understanding of human limitations; from this grows the capacity to be in awe of whatever we believe lies outside our control—God, truth, justice, nature, even death. The capacity for awe, as it grows, brings with it the capacity for respecting fellow human beings, flaws and all."

Woodruff clarifies his definition of reverence by contrasting reverence with faith. "Reverence is not faith," Woodruff says, "because the faithful may hold their faith with arrogance and self-satisfaction, and because the reverent may not know what to believe." While reverence requires belief in something beyond the self, it's still at odds with certain expressions of faith. Woodruff says, "If a religious group thinks it speaks and acts as God commands in all things, this is a failure of reverence." Such a self-assured faith destroys reverence.

By contrast, as we reflect on death, we realize we cannot control it. This powerlessness inspires a certain awe. What follows is a new respect for all human beings—the rich, the poor, the famous, the corrupt, the noble. All are bound by death. We have no room for pride.

Indeed, Woodruff claims that "an irreverent soul is unable to feel respect for people it sees as lower than itself—ordinary people, prisoners, children." In other words, the understanding that none of us is all-powerful or all-knowing inspires reverence. We're all vulnerable, all fallible.

Woodruff also claims that "reverence runs across religions and even outside them through the fabric of any community, however secular. We may be divided from one another by our beliefs, but never by reverence." Woodruff adds, "If you desire peace in the world, do not pray that everyone share your beliefs. Pray instead that all may be reverent."

Again, we're united in reverence because we all know that we have at least one deep limitation in common with each other—death. While none of us knows for certain what happens after death, we—*all of us*, Mormon and non-Mormon alike—know at least that we have death in common.

When we keep this in mind, we see that we shouldn't treat our relationships or our time lightly. We should internalize the fact that we might die at any moment, and then get to work as though we will live for a thousand years.

We should put reverence into practice.

Part 2: How to Practice Reverence

Wayne Booth spent his life teaching how to practice reverence.

He served an LDS mission in Illinois during the 1940s even though he harbored serious doubts about the Church. Throughout his mission he worried whether he was doing any good. What right did he have to tell people what to believe when he wasn't even sure what he believed himself?

To overcome his anxiety, he decided that he would practice empathetic dialogue with people he met. To do this, Booth decided he would first listen to what others had to say about God and religion. Then, when he was sure he had heard and understood, he would tell them what he thought. He found that this practice opened up space to really connect with others, and he found peace in those connections regardless of whether he converted anyone to Mormonism.

Wayne Booth later studied rhetoric and went on to be a major influence in the field. Years after his mission, he thought about empathetic dialogue in rhetorical terms. He even coined an admittedly ugly (but useful!) word for it. He called it *rhetorology*, which comes from the Greek word for "speaker" (*rhetor*) and the Latin word for "study of" (*ology*). Rhetorology: The empathetic study of speakers.

Booth defined rhetorology as "the probing of the deepest convictions underlying both sides in any conflict." In other words, rhetorology has no concern for winning an argument. Those who practice rhetorology don't ask, "How can I persuade an opponent to my way of thinking?" but "How can I find common ground with my opponent so that we can move forward together?"[1]

This is a potentially painful practice. Rhetorology demands that you open yourself up to the possibility that your position is wrong. As Booth said, "Any genuine rhetorologist entering any fray is committed to the possibility of conversion to the 'enemy' camp." That is, practicing rhetorology means that both sides openly admit the weak points of their own positions to their rivals. This openness allows 'rivals' to genuinely listen to each other.

Let's look at two examples of how rhetorology might work in practice.

1. Don and Cherie

Don and Cherie are active Mormons who have been happily married for 12 years and have 3 kids.

Recently, Don has been reading more about Mormon history online. He has come to the conclusion that some aspects of the Church's teachings aren't true.

He tries to tell Cherie what he has found, but whenever he brings up a controversial topic, she shuts down. Instead she bears her testimony and tells Don she doesn't want to hear anything more about the subject.

At first Don turns combative. He continues to bring up all the messy details from his research, even against Cherie's wishes. Every time he does this, she feels angry and hurt, and the conversations go nowhere. For two weeks every interaction between Don and Cherie is tense.

Then Don tries a different approach—an approach centered on vulnerability, empathy, and love. He sits down with Cherie and asks her to help him list all the beliefs or values they still have in common.

At first Cherie resists, but when Don starts listing some of their commonalities, she joins in. They find that they both want the best for their kids, they both enjoy (most of) the people in their ward, they both have had profound spiritual experiences in Mormonism, they both feel a need to serve in their community, they both like singing in the ward choir, and so on. By the time the list reaches 20 or 30 common beliefs or values, the anxiety that had pervaded the house diminishes.

Then Don asks Cherie to explain her opinion about his new beliefs as honestly as she can. As Cherie does this, Don listens. He doesn't turn combative or tell her that she is closed-minded or that she misunderstands him. He just listens.

Then Don writes out Cherie's position as best he can and asks her if he's accurately captured her feelings. She reads what he wrote, changes a few words, and then says that she feels understood.

From there Don asks if he can explain his position. At first Cherie says no, but when Don says that he won't go into the uncomfortable details of Church history again, that he just wants to talk about his thoughts and feelings in general terms, she says yes. So Don explains that he wants to live a quality life with Cherie and their kids, that he wants to be a better husband and father, and that he is trying his best to be earnest and objective in studying Church history.

When Don is done, Cherie writes out his position as best she can. Don feels understood.

From there, they revisit their list of common goals and decide to be more deliberate about meeting those goals. They commit to spending more quality time with their kids and serving more frequently in their community.

Over the next few weeks, Don realizes that he had been arguing on the level of truth while Cherie had been arguing on the level of beauty. He wanted her to get the facts straight (as he understood them) while she wanted him to bring peace into their home. They were speaking past each other. As Don learns to bring peace into the house, he builds trust with Cherie. Their relationship improves, even though Don still has doubts about certain Mormon truth claims.

It takes a few years, but eventually Cherie is willing to fully explore the Church's truth claims and come to her own conclusions.

Do Don and Cherie stay in the Church, or do they leave?

Answering that question is not the point of the story. The point is that as Don and Cherie practice empathetic dialogue, they move in a positive direction together, whatever that direction might be for them. They move closer to living a quality life.

2. Stephen and Brad

Stephen has recently left the Church and has been posting angry things about Mormonism on Facebook. His long-time friend Brad grows increasingly weary of Stephen's posts. Stephen does not seem to consider his friendship with Brad. He writes that Mormonism is a force for evil in the world and that people who still belong to the Church are ignorant bigots who can't think for themselves.

At first Brad thinks about simply de-friending Stephen—or at least hiding his posts. But as he reflects on their friendship, Brad decides it's worth saving. They've known each other for years: they grew up in the same ward and had many similar interests. Brad reaches out to Stephen via a personal message.

Brad writes that he saw Stephen's post and is curious about what instigated it. Stephen responds with a list of grievances. He doesn't like how the Church spends its money on things like City Creek Center in Salt Lake City, or how the Church mistreats gays and lesbians. Brad says he'd like to understand Stephen's position better and invites him to go camping—something they used to do often before they came to different conclusions about Mormonism. Stephen accepts the offer.

While camping, Brad asks Stephen about his journey out of Mormonism, including his struggles. In the past, Brad would've made a series of curt responses to all of Stephen's negative assertions about the Church. This time he simply listens, letting Stephen tell his story from beginning to end as he might do if he were being interviewed on a podcast. When Stephen finishes, Brad says that he can understand why Stephen feels the way he does—and he means it. Brad even feels a bit irritated at the Church for some of the things Stephen brought up. He realizes there are legitimate ways that Mormonism can and should improve.

However, Brad still believes that Stephen's mean-spirited Facebook posts do more harm than good. He thinks the posts hurt people and close down conversation.

So Brad asks Stephen what he thinks they still have in common even if they've reached different conclusions about Mormonism. At first Stephen struggles to list anything, but as Brad starts listing things—camping, science fiction, the Beatles, etc.—

Stephen starts to remember moments from their past. Many of these moments occurred during church activities. The more Stephen reflects, the more he realizes that many of the people in their ward growing up were genuinely trying to do good.

Stephen and Brad move beyond their differences and spend the rest of the night sitting around the campfire recalling crazy stories about Scout camp.

Again, the point of this story isn't about whether Stephen comes back to Mormonism or whether Brad leaves. Rather the point is that empathetic dialogue can save relationships and lead to a quality life.

***

These two stories show that rhetorology is grounded in an understanding of human limitations. They illustrate that rhetorology is reverence in practice.

Reverence and Rhetorology Lead to Truth, Beauty, and Goodness

All this talk about reverence and rhetorology might make it seem like I've forgotten about truth, beauty, and goodness. In reality, reverence and rhetorology are how we find each of these ideals.

How do we find truth? By starting from the assumption that we could be wrong and by listening—*really* listening—to the views of those who disagree with us. From there, we see where we can agree and try, however clumsily, to move forward together.

How do we find beauty? By starting from a position of vulnerability. If we enter every conversation with the knowledge that we could be wrong, we'll find that our conversations often bring profound peace. In addition, cultivating an attitude of reverence is literally the process of cultivating beauty. They're synonymous.

How do we find goodness? Again, we must acknowledge that we could be wrong—or at least we must acknowledge that there are different ways to be good. Not everyone subscribes to your ideology, and that's okay. We need a multiplicity of methods to find collective goodness.

Rhetorology is at the heart of truth, beauty, and goodness. It also enables us to have empathy for other people.

As we feel empathy, we can't help but love each other—even those we may have thought of as lost or wayward. Even those we may have thought of as enemies. We have no room for pride or arrogance. No room to divide the world into sheep and goats.

And so we must learn to save our relationships. We must learn to love, even when we disagree. This pure love is the fruit of the pursuit of truth, beauty, and goodness. It should be our goal, whether or not we remain Mormon.

Part 3: Eternal Progression
"What we do now echoes in eternity."
—Marcus Aurelius

As I draw to the end of this book, I want to tell a universal story—a story that transcends religious belief. For all the upsides of religion, one of the downsides is that it can make us think we're living separate stories. In its least inspired moments, religion convinces us that there's the story of the righteous and the story of the outsider. In this narrative, if you're not one of the righteous, you're a lost cause. My mission president used to say that nothing of significance happens in a person's life until they are baptized, a sentiment that epitomizes many of the worst aspects of religious belief.

But the real story is about us—humanity—striving together for survival and evolution. In one sense, this story fits with the Mormon belief that we are all gods in embryo, on a path toward eternal progression. Even if you don't believe this concept literally, we should all believe that we're on a path of upward evolution. As a species we're striving to be something bigger and better than what we are. We should realize that all of us—those who have lived, those who live now, and those who will live—are part of the same story, the same effort. The human race is headed toward greatness that we cannot comprehend.

Just think of how far we've come in the past 300 years. We've lengthened lifespans, illegalized slavery, landed on the Moon, created a way to communicate instantly around the globe, and so much more.

How much further along will we be 100 years from now? How about 1,000 years from now? 10,000? Will we find the cure to cancer? Will we map the depths of the ocean? Will we venture to other planets? Will we discover planets with sentient life on them? Will we find answers to the grandest mysterious of life?

I believe that given time we will find these things. I believe the answers will consistently surprise us.

In the meantime we must be part of the solution.

This means, first of all, that we must do our part to bring humanity closer to truth, beauty, and goodness. As I outlined in the introduction, we each have something different to offer on this front. Whether you're inspired by intellectual curiosity, experiencing beauty, or communities that fight for moral causes, you can be part of the solution by developing your strengths and maintaining a blend of truth, beauty, and goodness that sits right with you.

Second, and perhaps most urgently on a global scale, we must do our part to make sure humans are still around for centuries to come. There are so many ways we could go wrong. We could ruin the planet through pollution, overexploitation, or nuclear warfare. It doesn't take a scientist to understand that even our most common habits are unsustainable. We can't consume fossil fuels forever. We can't continue to dump millions of tons of garbage into landfills. We can't keep killing other species as fast as we are without forever changing the ecosystem and hurting our chances of survival. It's unsustainable.[2] We must reform our habits if we want to survive as a species. We can't treat the planet like it was made for this generation alone.

Two Options Going Forward

Having said all of this, what should we do going forward as it relates to Mormonism?

I'll touch on two options in closing. These options aren't mutually exclusive, nor are they the only options. Each path depends on a range of personal situations and beliefs.

Option #1

Stay in Mormonism. Know that individuals and institutions will continue to improve as we improve. Stay with the hope that Mormonism will get better at pursuing truth, beauty, and goodness. Stay with the notion that you can help it change.

I'm sympathetic to this option. I'm the product of two families whose Mormon ties go back to the pioneers. There's nothing I can do to change that, so why not embrace it? Mormonism is in my blood. It *is* me. In some sense, no matter what I believe I will always be Mormon since I've actively lived as a Mormon my whole life.

There are many upsides to staying in the Church. You'll have a ready-made community and an agreed-upon canon. Also, you'll be part of a legacy that has perhaps been part of your family for centuries.

There are possible downsides, as well. You might find it difficult to engage in conversations where your underlying assumptions about the world are dramatically different from other members. You might also feel uncomfortable participating in a community that promotes ideas you disagree with—such as treatment of the LGBT community. Finally, you might feel anxiety about your standing in the Church. You might worry that you're on the cusp of excommunication for saying the wrong thing in public. In such cases, you might find that as much as you like certain aspects of Mormonism, you're better off not participating.

My hope is that the Church will live by the words of Joseph F. Smith when he said, "So long as a man believes in God and has a little faith in the Church organization, we nurture and aid that person to continue faithfully as a member of the Church though he may not believe all that is revealed." Depending on how we define *God*, the kind of Mormonism that Joseph F. Smith describes could include just about everyone.

Option #2
Join with people who pursue truth, beauty, and goodness inside and outside of Mormonism. Build new communities that are centered on timeless ideals—communities that push at the envelope of individual and institutional progress.

You might join a more progressive religious community such as the Unitarians or join a meditation community such as Lower Lights Sangha in Salt Lake City. Or you might join one of the post-religious communities that have sprung up around the world, including the School of Life, Sunday Assembly, Secular Buddhism, and Oasis. These secular groups aim to replicate the functions of religion without metaphysical claims about God and angels. By joining these communities, you will be a pioneer in a new tradition that will likely continue in some form for centuries to come.

The upsides are that you might feel empowered to speak out about what you really believe. You might also create friendships with people whose beliefs are closer to your own. In addition, you might find that the lessons and activities of a secular group are more meaningful to you personally.

The downsides are that newly formed communities can be hard to navigate. You'll find that people in these communities still disagree—sometimes stridently—about what to believe and how to implement those beliefs. You might also find that it's difficult for secular groups to define themselves in positive terms instead of merely being nonreligious. Finally, you may find that there are aspects of Mormonism (such as regular meeting times, a predictable structure, or familiar hymns) that you didn't fully appreciate before trying to launch something new.

Having said all of that, I personally would love to see more of these secular groups flourish. They serve an urgent and needed purpose for an increasingly secular society.

***

Whatever option you choose, you don't have to reinvent your life from scratch. You don't have to retreat from everything in your past. Instead you can take your evolution slowly and hold onto whatever is true, beautiful, and good. You can grow in a way that is productive and healthy.

My hope is that our community—full of orthodox, unorthodox, and former Mormons—will navigate toward a more vibrant future. My hope is that we will learn to love the people we disagree with. My hope is that we will each leave the world a better place for the generations that follow. My hope, finally, is that we will use the framework of truth, beauty, and goodness as a way to find common ground, save our relationships, and seek a quality life.

The End

Thank you for reading *When Mormons Doubt*. I hope you found the book to be helpful in your efforts to save your relationships and seek a quality life.

If you did, please consider leaving a review on Amazon.com. I would appreciate it tremendously.

If you didn't, I'd love to hear your thoughts. Feel free to email me at ogden.jon@gmail.com. I'm interested in refining the message in this book.

Thanks!

Jon Ogden

Recommended Reading

In no particular order, here are 20 books I would recommend if you want to know more about the topics I've explored here. Each of these books has changed my life for the better.

The Righteous Mind, Jonathan Haidt
Meditations, Marcus Aurelius
A Guide to the Good Life, William Irvine
My Many Selves, Wayne Booth
A Brief History of Thought, Luc Ferry
The Consolations of Philosophy, Alain de Botton
The Swerve, Stephen Greenblatt
Doubt: A History, Jennifer Hecht
The Varieties of Religious Experience, William James
The Tao Te Ching, Lao Tzu
10% Happier, Dan Harris
The Gospel According to Jesus, Stephen Mitchell
Meeting Jesus Again for the First Time, Marcus Borg
Power of the Parable, John Dominic Crossan
A History of God, Karen Armstrong
The History of Western Philosophy, Bertrand Russell
In the Realm of Hungry Ghosts, Gabor Mate
Navigating Mormon Faith Crisis, Thomas McConkie
Living the Secular Life, Phil Zuckerman
Rough Stone Rolling, Richard Bushman

Acknowledgements

When I started this book, I figured it would take me about six months at most. Instead it took three years. During that time I had help from a long list of friends and family—only a portion of which I'll be able to thank here.

First, I need to thank my amazing wife, who is a phenomenal reader and writer and who has not one but *two* master's degrees. She helped with every draft in between running marathons and having a baby, and she deserves credit for bringing this project to completion.

Second, I'm grateful to my long-time friend, Drew Vernon, who introduced me to many of the nuances of Mormon history, who read drafts, and who was always there to bounce ideas off of. He's one of the smartest and most generous people I know.

Third, I'd like to thank my family—my parents and sisters. They too read drafts and were fabulous sounding boards. They've been terrific examples when it comes to being kind to people whose religious beliefs differ from their own.

Finally, I'd like to thank others who were involved in reading drafts and talking about ideas, including Anthony Garrett, Jeremy Walker, Dustin Grady, Paul Malan, Amy Johnson Despain, Jeff Swift, Laura Summerhays, Trevor Bodily, Ryan White, and so many more.

It turns out that writing a book is a much more ambitious project than I had supposed, and I couldn't have done it alone.

Endnotes

_____

Introduction

[1] LDS.org/topics/essays

[2] Three things: 1) If the word "spiritual" bothers you, feel free to use a more secular version of the idea such as the "higher emotions." 2) Stephen Covey puts *service* in the category of spiritual health. I can see where he's coming from (service brings spiritual feelings), but in this book I primarily thinking of service as belonging to the realm of goodness. 3) My definition of goodness expands beyond social health to include all actions that lead to wellbeing.

[3] Other approximate descriptions for truth, beauty, and goodness might include:
- Epistemology, aesthetics, and ethics
- Logos, pathos, and ethos
- Science, art, morality
- The head, the heart, and the hands

[4] Alexander, Bruce. "The Myth of Drug-Induced Addiction." Parliament of Canada, n.d.

Hari, Johann. *Chasing the Scream: The First and Last Days of the War on Drugs.* New York: Bloomsbury, 2015.

Mate, Gabor. *In the Realm of Hungry Ghosts.* Knopf, 2008

Beauty, Part One

[1] Booth, Wayne. *My Many Selves: A Quest for a Plausible Harmony.* Logan: USU Press, 2006.

[2] Friedrich Nietzsche, whom I'm generally reluctant to quote since he's more of a provocateur than a seeker of truth, beauty, and goodness.

[3] Here are some books that can help you get started with a mindfulness practice:

Harris, Dan. *10% Happier: How I Tamed the Voice in My Head, Reduced Stress Without Losing My Edge, and Found Self-Help That Actually Works—A True Story.* It Books, 2014.

Tolle, Eckhart. *The Power of Now: A Guide to Spiritual Enlightenment.* Namaste Publishing, 2004. (Note that, as with many people deeply invested in mindfulness, Eckhart Tolle occasionally veers toward unscientific claims—something to ignore.)

Singer, Michael. *The Untethered Soul: The Journey Beyond Yourself.* New Harbinger Publications, 2007.

Hanh, Thich Nhat. *The Miracle of Mindfulness: An Introduction to the Practice of Meditation.* Beacon Press, 1999.

Because beauty is an experience, reading books is insufficient when it comes to learning how to practice mindfulness. I therefore also recommend finding an instructor you trust. For those of you in Utah, I recommend Thomas Wirthlin McConkie and Noah Rasheta. I've taken multiple workshops from both of them, and I highly recommend the experience.

In addition, I also subscribe to Calm.com, which has a series of guided meditations.

[4] This is from a fantastic Facebook group named "A Thoughtful Faith." If you have doubts but are still interested in making Mormonism work, check it out. It's my favorite LDS-related forum, full of wonderful people.

Goodness, Part One
[1] The full quote from Epicurus reads, "There are times when we pass over many pleasures, whenever greater difficulty follows from them. Also, we regard many pains as better than pleasures, since a greater pleasure will attend us after we have endured pain for a long time."

Epicurus. *The Essential Epicurus*. Trans. Eugene O'Connor. Prometheus Books, 1993. Note that the other quotations from Epicurus also come from this source.

[2] Epictetus. *The Handbook*.

[3] Seneca. *Letters*.

[4] Andrews, Robert. *The Columbia Dictionary of Quotations*. Columbia, 1993.

[5] We might say that beauty is subjective, goodness is inter-subjective, and truth is objective.

[6] Some critics might say that Epicurus's formula isn't a sufficient model for goodness because it means that people who have clinical depression aren't good. This is a difficult critique to respond to. However, I would say that it's critical to separate sadness from depression. Sadness is treated with connection. Depression is a medical problem, no different from contracting the flu. We would never say that someone who contracts the flu is immoral, and we should extend the same compassion to people with clinical depression.

[7] Kierkegaard, Soren. *Either/Or.* 1843.

Truth, Part One

[1] U.S. National Archives. "From George Washington to Officers of the Army, 15 March 1783."

[2] Tucker, David. *Enlightened Republicanism: A Study of Jefferson's Notes on the State of Virginia.* Lexington Books, 2008.

[3] Haglund, Richard, and David Whittaker. "Intellectual History." Encyclopedia of Mormonism.

[4] Pomeroy, Steven Ross. "The Key to Science (and Life) Is Being Wrong." Scientific American, 13 November 2012.

Beauty, Part Two

[1] Quoted in William James's *Varieties of Religious Experience.*

[2] Rankin, Marianne. *An Introduction to Religious and Spiritual Experience.* A&C Black, 2008.

[3] Comte-Sponville, Andre. *The Little Book of Atheist Spirituality.* Penguin Books, 2008.

[4] Winfrey, Oprah. "What Oprah Knows for Sure About Stillness, Peace and Glorious Moments." May 2006.

[5] Carnegie, Dale. *How to Stop Worrying and Start Living.* Simon and Schuster, 2010.

[6] Quoted in William James's *Varieties of Religious Experience.*

[7] Rose, Charlie. "Paul Simon Interview," June 2007.

[8] Hsieh, Tony. Delivering Happiness: A Path to Profits, Passion, and Purpose. Grand Central Publishing, 2013.

[9] Vincent, Ken. *The Golden Thread: God's Promise of Universal Salvation.* iUniverse, 2005.

[10] Taylor, Jill Bolte. "My Stroke of Insight." TED, 2008.

[11] Mitchell, Edgar. *The Way of the Explorer: An Apollo Astronaut's Journey Through the Material and Mystical Worlds.* ReadHowYouWant.com, 2009.

[12] Tagholm, Roger. "Face to Faith." *The Guardian*, 6 November 2009.

Goodness, Part Two

[1] Haidt, Jonathan. *The Righteous Mind: Why Good People Are Divided by Politics and Religion.* Vintage, 2013.

[2] Kling, Arnold. *The Three Languages of Politics.* Amazon Digital Services, 2013.

[3] Lipka, Michael. "U.S. Religious Groups and their Political Leanings." Pew Research, 2016.

Truth, Part Two

[1] LDS.org/topics/essays

[2] Here is a list of resources for people who would like to read faith-affirming texts about hard Mormon questions:

Givens, Terryl, and Fiona Givens. *The Crucible of Doubt: Reflections on the Quest for Faith.* Deseret Book Company, 2014.

Mason, Patrick. *Planted: Belief and Belonging in an Age of Doubt.* Deseret Book, 2015.

Ash, Michael R. *Shaken Faith Syndrome: Strengthening One's Testimony in the Face of Criticism and Doubt.* Provo: F.A.I.R., 2013.

Hales, Laura Harris. *A Reason for Faith: Navigating LDS Doctrine and Church History.* Salt Lake City: Deseret Book, 2016.

McConkie, Thomas. *Navigating Mormon Faith Crisis: A Simple Developmental Map.* Mormon Stages, 2015.

Miller, Adam S. *Letters to a Young Mormon.* Provo: Neal A. Maxwell Institute for Religious Scholarship, 2013.

Peck, Stephen L. *Evolving Faith: Wanderings of a Mormon Biologist.* Provo: Neal A. Maxwell Institute for Religious Scholarship, 2015.

Bushman, Richard L. *Joseph Smith: Rough Stone Rolling.* New York: Vintage, 2007.

[3] Runnells, Jeremy. "Letter to a CES Director."

[4] Mormon Quotes. MormonThink.com — See Birth Control, Evolution, Blacks, United States vs. the Mormons.

[5] Peterson, Daniel. "Richard Bushman and the fundamental claims of Mormonism." July 2016.

Goodness, Part Three

[1] "Religion in Everyday Life." Pew Research Center, 12 April 2016.

[2] Brooks, Arthur. *Who Really Cares? The Surprising Truth About Compassionate Conservatism.* Basic Books, 2007.

Putnam, Robert, and David Campbell. *American Grace: How Religion Divides and Unites Us.* Simon & Schuster, 2012.

[3] Gebauer, Jochen, Constantine Sedikides and Wiebke Neberich. "Religiosity, Social Self-Esteem, and Psychological Adjustment." *Psychological Science*, 2012.

[4] Zuckerman, Phil. *Living the Secular Life: New Answers to Old Questions.* Penguin Press, 2014.

Beauty, Part Three

[1] James, William. *The Varieties of Religious Experience.* 1902.

[2] Ibid.

[3] Ibid.

[4] Hallett, Garth. *A Middle Way to God.* Oxford University Press, 2000.

[5] Collins, Francis. *The Language of God: A Scientist Presents Evidence for Belief.* Simon and Schuster, 2008.

[6] Askreality. "My LDS Journey – Follow the Spirit." YouTube, 2014.

[7] Ibid.

[8] "Another Story of Conversion." *BecomingJewish.net*, 12 November 2015.

[9] Osgood, Kelsey. "Judaism and the Twice-Born." *NewYorker.com*, 1 April 2015.

[10] Lehorla 1. "Spiritual Witness." Youtube. Youtube, 22 October 2015.

[11] Ibid.

[12] Ibid.

[13] Ibid.

[14] Jonestown Transcript. *PBS.org*, 2013.

Truth, Part Three

[1] Byrne, Brian Patrick, et al. "All The People God Kills In The Bible." Vocativ, 20 April 2016.

[2] King, Martin Luther Jr. "The Autobiography of Martin Luther King, Jr." Ed. Clayborne Carson. Warner Books, reprinted 2001.

[3] Ehrman, Bart. *Misquoting Jesus: The Story Behind Who Changed the Bible and Why.* HarperOne. 2007

[4] Fisk, Bruce. "'Anti-Judaism' in the Gospel of John." Westmont College, n.d.

[5] Crossan, John D. The Power of Parable: How Fiction by Jesus Became Fiction about Jesus. New York: Harper One, 2013.

[6] Borg, Marcus. *Jesus: The Life, Teachings, and Relevance of a Religious Revolutionary.* Harper One. 2015

[1] Booth, Wayne. *The Rhetoric of Rhetoric: The Quest for Effective Communication.* Wiley-Blackwell, 2004.

[2] Ceballos, Gerardo, Paul Ehrlich, Anthony Barnosky, Andrés García, Robert M. Pringle and Todd M. Palmer. "Accelerated modern human–induced species losses: Entering the sixth mass extinction." Science Advances, 19 Jun 2015.

Made in the USA
Las Vegas, NV
21 March 2022

46077742R00098